R E D D E E R

BY

RICHARD JEFFERIES

AUTHOR OF

"THE GAMEKEEPER AT HOME" "WILD LIFE IN A SOUTHERN COUNTY"
"THE STORY OF MY HEART : MY AUTOBIOGRAPHY" ETC.

SECOND EDITION

WITH ILLUSTRATIONS BY MR. JOHN CHARLTON

HALSGROVE

First published by Longmans, Green and Co. 1884
Second edition 1892

Reprinted in facsimile, with a new introduction,
by Halsgrove 2001
Introduction © Victor Bonham-Carter 2001

ISBN 1 84114 120 8

Printed in Great Britain by Cromwell Printers Ltd,
Trowbridge

CONTENTS

RED DEER LAND.

INTRODUCTION *by Victor Bonham-Carter*

RICHARD Jefferies was born on 6 November 1848 at Coate, then a small farm about 2½ miles outside Swindon on the road to Marlborough. The house was thatched (later replaced by tiles) with two rooms on the ground floor, four on the first floor, and two large garrets in the roof. The kitchen was at the back of the house. There was a small flower garden, a vegetable patch, and several fruit trees. Apart from a few outbuildings and a handful of labourers' cottages, Coate was no more than a hamlet, little disturbed by traffic.

Richard Jefferies was the second of five children (three sons, two daughters), the family and household described, part-fact part-fiction in *Amaryllis at the Fair* (1887). 'Farmer Iden' was drawn from Richard's father, a true son of the soil, who wore rags to work in, kept a handful of spuds in his pocket and, after Sunday dinner of a leg of lamb, slept by the fire. His wife was scornful and mimicked his Wiltshire accent.

The farm was too small to survive as an independent holding and had eventually to be sold, though not before Richard had started work as a journalist and was able to pay his way. Before then, at the age of nine, he attended a day school in Swindon and began to read every book he could beg or borrow, but he also enjoyed playing with his chums on Coate Reservoir nearby (now an urban Nature Reserve within the boundaries of Swindon itself). This was the origin of *Bevis* (1882), a boys' adventure book. He also explored the downland, peopled with ancient castles and camps, and let his imagination rip over the landscape towards the Valley of the White Horse. One day someone said to an acquaintance, 'see 'ort on the downs?', and was told 'only Dick Jefferies moonin' about'.

Thanks to his friendship with a William Morris, a local man, his first literary adviser, who gave him the run of his library, Richard got his first job as a reporter on the *North Wilts Herald,* a new Conservative paper published in Swindon. This gave him a small income and the means to learn the trade of journalism. He was also trying to break into the wider publications market as a freelance, and wrote pieces on local and natural history, archaeology, and related subjects, which prompted him to explore the countryside as far as he could go.

In 1867-8 he was laid low by fever and returned to Coate to recover slowly, though life had horizons of brightness such as when he began his courtship of Miss Jessie Baden, who lived on a neighbouring farm.

In due course she became his wife. In periods of exhaustion and depression, he often turned to his aunt, Mrs Harrild, at Sydenham, who proved a true friend. By 1870 he had saved enough money to visit Brussels, a very smart capital city, and where he saw some of the wounded returning from the Battle of Sedan. By 1872 he was again in full flood of work, paid and unpaid, which included a venture into fiction. Over the next few years he wrote several novels with succulent titles, e.g. *The Scarlet Shawl* (1870), *Restless Human Hearts* (1875), *World's End* (1877), *Greene Fern Farm* (1880), and *Wood Magic* (1881). Though fiction was natural to him, for he had a vivid imagination, he was no novelist. His style was cumbered with clichés and sentimental situations to the extent that his novels can be written off as failures. His ability, however, to dream and convey his dreams in words found lively expression in two quite different books, *The Story of My Heart – My Autobiography* (1883) and *After London or Wild England* (1885). *The Story of My Heart* is a work of personal philosophy, expressed in poetic prose, beautifully written but, perhaps, just not able to sustain its mystic message, though it yielded some memorable passages. *After London or Wild England* is a fantasy. Part I describes an immense flood that engulfed London and the south of England, which thereafter reverted to marsh and jungle. 'Thames and Severn over-flowed and made an inland sea between the Cotswolds and the Downs, for the ruins of London blocked the river which changed into swamp'. Had Richard been writing in the winter of 2000-2001, he would hardly have felt it necessary to draw on his imagination, the flooded landscape would have lain before him. In the book, life reverted to barbarism, the islands that stood above the waters being inhabited by tramps and gypsies. Part II is a romance, centred upon Felix, who recovers much of the 'old knowledge' and prefers study to war. As Edward Thomas says in his book about Jefferies, this is in a sense a sequel to *Bevis*. Instead of Richard sailing and fishing on Coate Water, this is about an inland sea on which Felix may sail alone and seek adventure.

In February 1872 Joseph Arch had 'mounted his pigstool under the chestnut at Wellesbourne' and founded the first successful farm workers' union. Members from Warwickshire and other Midland counties struck work, asking for 16 instead of 12 shillings a week. They were refused. This prompted Richard to write three historic letters to *The Times* about the Wiltshire Labourer in November of that year which were 'conspicuous for lucid, forcible and simple exposition' of a subject he knew at first hand. They constitute a social document, were widely read, and encouraged Richard, at this early date and possibly unwisely, to freelance as a rural commentator and recorder. It enabled him to contribute a number of articles to national as well as regional journals, such as *The Pall Mall Gazette, Manchester Guardian, Graphic, National Review, Standard,* et al. A number of these pieces were duly collected and issued in volume form, e.g. *The Gamekeeper at Home* (1878), *Wild Life in a Southern County* (1879), *Hodge and his Masters* (1880), *Round about a Great Estate* (1880), *The Life of the Fields* (1884), *The Open Air* (1885), and *Field and Hedgerow* (1889) – the latter contained his 'Last Essays', collected by his widow, and who chose the title. It is a remarkable fact that, in a short life of barely thirty-eight years, Richard had 22 books to his credit.

This brings us to Richard's book about Exmoor – *Red Deer* (1884). What prompted him to visit the area in June 1882 is not clear. For him however it was a short period of freedom from ill health, and a chance to see a region of a highly distinctive character. He wrote:

It is a minute account of the natural history of the wild deer of Exmoor and of the mode of hunting them. I went all over the area a short while since, first in order to see the deer for myself; and in addition I had the advantage of getting full information from the huntsman himself and from others who have watched the deer for twenty years past. The chase of the wild stag is a bit out of the life of the fifteenth century brought down to our own time.

Richard was referring to the help given him by Arthur Heal, huntsman to the Devon and Somerset Staghounds, who lived at North Ley, and by his bachelor son, Fred, who owned several farms round Exford. Advice from such sources could not go wrong. This is a straightforward work of reportage – factual, orderly and consistent. He described the landscape – no sharp mountain peaks, but a tableland of undulating hills covered with heather, moorland grasses and fern, intersected by deep narrow valleys with streams and trees.

As to the deer, the stags are remarkable in that they lose their antlers every spring, the new growth being covered with a skin called 'velvet', until about midsummer when this dries out and becomes hard; but it also causes intense irritation so that the stag rubs its head against bushes or trees for relief. The new antlers are a formidable weapon used to ward off other stags when competing for mating with the hinds. At this time of year, usually

October, stag hunting is stopped for a few weeks, and the woods resound with 'belling' or roaring , which is the stag's war cry to discourage competitors. The life of the stag is so bound up with its antlers that it may be said to begin and end with them. There is no more beautiful creature than a stag in his pride of antler, his coat of ruddy gold, his grace of form and motion. It is an odd thing, but relatively few antlers are found, even by gamekeepers and shepherds who keep a keen look-out – for, when found, a good pair will sell for £5 or £10.

Without stag hunting, there would be absolutely nothing doing about Exmoor – no life, no movement. Red deer are a passion with both rich and poor. Farmers, large and small, hunt, and many follow on foot. The damage done by deer to crops and gardens is so extensive that, without the goodwill of the farming community, hunting would not last a single season. Compensation is of course paid, but can never make good the loss of a crop, which includes the market value of the crop itself, and the residual value of the fertiliser expended. Moreover deer are wasteful creatures, taking one bite and throwing the rest away.

Richard Jefferies died in his late thirties in 1887, after years of torturing illness diagnosed as 'chronic fibroid phthisis'. Earlier in December 1881, when ill with fistula, he described the pain like 'lightning through the brain' and underwent four operations in the course of a year. They were probably the first symptoms of the illness that killed him. When recommended to apply to the Royal Literary Fund for a grant to pay for medicine and a trip abroad, he rejected the idea with contumely, 'because he believed that the Fund was maintained by Dukes and Marquises, instead of authors and journalists and publishers'. Despite bouts of pain, his will power, his intense interest in the subject, his industry and – as Richard Church thought – his extraordinary power of physical vision enabled him to produce a body of work which, in terms of both quantity and quality, few other writers about the countryside have been able to attain.

After the Second World War, Samuel Looker edited and Lutterworth republished several titles, and Looker also assembled a book about Richard's *Notebooks*. This is a pattern likely to be repeated in some form every decade or so, for Richard Jefferies will always find a place in the history of English literature.

RED DEER.

I.

RED DEER LAND.

THE wild red deer in the West of England
have so largely increased in numbers recently
as to occupy a very different and far more
important position in the fauna of the
country than used to be the case. Almost
every one has heard as a kind of tradition
that the red deer which used to roam in the
forests all over England still remained wild
in a corner of Somerset. The circumstance
is often alluded to in books and conversa-
tion as an interesting story, not much more
real than the adventures of Leather-stocking

A

among the Red Indians and deer of the backwoods. Or, if accepted as a fact, it is looked at in the same light as the preservation of white wild cattle in certain parks, wild but protected by enclosure. Those, of course, who have hunted in Somerset are well acquainted with the truth, but to the majority of people the red deer of Exmoor are like the golden eagles shot from time to time as they pass over southern woods, and preserved as valuable curiosities. Although so many tourists visit Somerset and Devon, and go through the red deer country, their objects are generally scenery or trout-fishing, and they are there at a season when the deer are peculiarly shy and seldom seen. Nor, if seen, could a casual passer-by understand the full meaning of their appearance. They are associated with the deer kept in parks, and considered to be wild only in a limited sense.

ENTERING ORCHARDS. — *Page* 5.

In reality the red deer are wild in the fullest sense of the term, as wild and unrestrained in their movements as the deer of the backwoods of America. If found in one spot to-day, they may be miles distant on the morrow. They roam over hill and moor, through valley and plain, wood, meadow, and cultivated field, entering orchards, gardens, and allotments from time to time during the night, exactly as wild animals do about the settlements of colonists. They are never supplied with food even in the severest winters, but find their "meat" where they can, like the hares. The hunt is no paper chase—no artificial sport, like that of deer turned out from a cart—the hunt is a real chase of the most arduous character, and for the purpose of killing the stag or hind, which is afterwards eaten as venison. The pursuit is attended with great fatigue and considerable danger, that of the hind,

which is followed in winter, especially re-
quiring hardihood and endurance. In distant countries wild animals are hunted in
order to diminish their numbers and the
damage they do to the crops of settlers ; and
in the same manner of recent seasons the
chase of the red deer has been directed to
the reduction of the herds. The object, it
must be borne in mind, is the actual killing
of the wild animal, not merely the riding
after it. There is in every respect an exact
parallel between the hunt in the days of
Chevy Chase and the hunt of the present
time.

These deer have been hitherto spoken of
as the red deer of Exmoor, but they have
now extended so widely, roaming over great
tracts of two counties, that this limited term
is no longer applicable. They are now the
red deer of the West of England. But
Exmoor was their retreat during the long,

long passage of time down from mediæval
days to our own, and it was from thence
that they spread abroad under favourable
conditions. It remains the centre of Red
Deer Land, and without a clear idea of
this remarkable district no one can com-
prehend how it is that the deer are so
really wild.

The moors of the Exe river are not flat
stretches of marshland, but hills of great
height covered with heather. The term
mountains may almost be applied to them
—numbers of the ridges are twice the height
of Beachy Head or the Dyke at Brighton—
Dunkery Beacon is three times as high. But
the conformation of the country is such that
on entering it the elevations do not seem
very unusual, for as it is all high and raised
the eye has nothing with which to contrast
it. When on the moor it appears an immense table-land, intersected by deep narrow

valleys, called coombes, at the bottom of
which a stream always flows. At some
distance apart are ranges of hills rising
gradually and with gentle slopes above the
general level of the moor. The curves appear so moderate and the ascent so easy
that there can be no difficulty in walking or
riding over them. Dunkery itself is nothing
more than an undulation, scarcely to be
separated at some points of view from the
common line of the ridge. These hills seem
only a mile or two away and within half-
an-hour's walk.

But on going towards them, the table-land
suddenly sinks in a deep coombe, when it
is apparent that the moor which looked so
level is really the top of a hill. This
coombe has to be descended, and ascended,
and the sides are high and steep. Presently
another coombe intervenes, and after five
miles' walking very little progress has been

made. At last the slope of the hill is
reached, and has now expanded into a
mountainous ascent, not to be overcome
without much labour and more time. The
country is, in fact, very deceptive, much
wider, and much more difficult than it looks.
The expanse confuses the eye, and will not
allow it to judge distances. From the spot
where you stand to the range yonder is perhaps five-and-twenty miles. On Haddon
Hill the glance passes from Dunkery, which
overlooks the Severn Sea, to Sidmouth Gap
by St. George's Channel, so that the eye
sees across the entire breadth of England
there.

The consequence of these great distances
is that all minor distances are shrunken,
and five miles looks nothing. The illusion
is assisted by the smooth outline of the
moors, without a fence for miles together,
and without a visible tree, for the covers

are in the coombes, and there are few or no copses on the hills, as in the South Downs. Nothing whatever breaks up the surface and measures the view. Heather covers the largest part of the ground, which is never ploughed or sown, and where there are no flower-grown meads. One vast breadth of open, wild, and treeless country reaches in every direction, and it is at once obvious why the deer have remained at large since the most ancient times, for the land is in the same condition as it was centuries ago. The plough has not touched it, and civilisation has not come near.

This day may be in the reign of Charles the First or Queen Elizabeth, or even in the Plantagenet times, for aught the appearance of the land says to the contrary. The cross-bow, the cloth-yard arrow, or the clumsy matchlock may still be in use—armour may be worn—and manuscripts be as yet un-

supplanted by printed books. There is no
printing-press here—the moor has known no
change ; it is the home of the wild red deer,
their home since William the Conqueror
landed, and long before then—since Roman
arms and Roman money ruled the island
beyond the ocean.

Why has Exmoor remained in this condition, uncultivated for so many centuries?
why does it still defy agriculture and improvement? Three causes present themselves—the nature of the soil, the cost of
labour, and the character of the climate.
A long winter of eight months, with continuous rains and heavy fogs, is succeeded by
a hot, short summer. Though the summer
is very hot there are occasional intervals of
cold. Sometimes when vapour is sweeping
over from the Severn Sea it is accompanied
by a wind which chills to the marrow. In
1882 there was quite a crust of frost on the

morning of June 21. When the sun shines
the fierce rays pour down on the heather
and dry it till it is hard and wiry, so hard
as to wear out the stoutest boots quickly.
Innumerable bees gather to the heather-
bells; it is a question where they all come
from; they must travel long distances to
the feast of honey. The whortleberries
ripen, and women and children go out to
pick them. It is their harvest of the year;
tons and tons—whole truck-loads—are sent
away by railroad. Rain and fog alternate
for most of the winter, together with intense cold. Against this bitter cold large
quantities of turf are laid in, and the fires
on the hearths banked up in glowing piles.

The thickness of the fogs often prevents
the sight from penetrating more than a few
yards, and so confuses the wayfarer that the
residents much prefer the darkness of night
to the vapours of noonday. They can find

their path by night, but the thick mist
sometimes defies even the shepherds. It
hangs for days ; Dunkery Beacon is hidden
in it when, at the same time, the vale beneath is clear and lit by the sun. It is
observed that when Dunkery Beacon is thus
completely covered the Selworthy range of
hills just opposite are frequently free of
fog. The staghounds are accordingly taken
across to Selworthy at such times. To
hunt on the moors about Dunkery is impossible—the hounds would be lost to view
in a moment in the vapour. Winds sweep
over the exposed heights sometimes with
such violence that a man can hardly retain
his seat in the saddle. Such inclemency
seems due to the elevation of the land, the
nearness of the Western sea, and the nature
of the soil, which retains water.

Good crops are obtained in the vales,
though everything is late in spring, so that

it is a matter of surprise so much can be grown in so short a time. Cost of labour must be understood to include cost of lime and haulage, as without lime the soil cannot be improved. This soil consists of a black friable peat, in some places deep, in others shallow. Under a hot sun it becomes dry, but during the winter, and indeed for the greater part of the year, it is soft and watery. Bogs are numerous, and springy places which are almost bogs. Labour must first be expended in clearing the surface of heather, whortleberries, and rough grass. Lime must then be carried up, and the cost of haulage equals the price of the material.

When ploughed and laid down to grass, unless broken up from time to time, the ground will revert and yield nothing but rushes. Acres upon acres may be seen covered with rushes where land has been reclaimed, and has reverted to waste. Yet it would seem that the black peaty earth contains the elements of fertility, and persons are continually tempted to lay out their money in an effort to do something with it. Here is, in fact, a great agricultural problem.

An immense experiment was made some years ago by the owner of a large part of the moors to improve his seventy thousand acres. He caused the surface to be broken up, and lime to be hauled. Walls were built to form enclosures, and when the deer climbed the walls wire was put along, in which wire many deer got hung by their legs, and had to be killed—being injured. A tramway was laid down. Instead of the horned mountain sheep, or " Porlocks," Cheviots were introduced. Numerous farmhouses were erected in a substantial manner, and fir copses planted to shelter the inmates and the stock in the yards from the tremendous gales. The land was let to Scotch farmers, who came down from the North to a country almost resembling their own. A mansion like a castle was built in the midst of the wilderness. All these measures were such as would naturally suggest themselves, but only partially succeeded.

The farmhouses are now occupied by Scotch shepherds; if you knock at the door a Scotch face appears, and you are offered a glass of milk, to which you are "varra" welcome. The boundless heather, the deep glens, and the red deer correspond to the Gaelic accent. The tramway is gone, and the track has disappeared for great part of its length under thick heather. Over the walls the deer climb easily, and the unfinished castle is moss-grown. All that remains is the improvement effected in some places by the mixture of lime and by the

efforts of the Northern farmers, some irri-
gated meadows in the glens, and the farmhouses at long intervals. So far as the
general vista—so far as the red deer and
the black game—are concerned, Exmoor has
not altered one iota. The vast moors have
simply swallowed up the efforts of man to
conquer them. The details of this experiment explain why Exmoor remains mediæval.
It resists the perpetual nibbling which goes
on around the inhabited places.

The villages and towns are far apart, the
towns are only so called as having markets,
and are no larger than the villages in corn
counties. These Exmoor villages are usually
situated at the bottom of deep coombes,
those coombes in which flow the largest
streams, as the Barle and Exe. For instance, Exford, which is the very centre of
Red Deer Land, and has been chosen for
the kennels of the staghounds, is on the

B

banks of the Exe in a deep hollow. It
is absolutely isolated. There is a well-
conducted hotel, the White Horse, where
huntsmen and trout-fishers find accommo-
dation, but it is ten miles to the nearest
station, and there is no telegraph. The
hamlet street is level for a little distance,
but with this exception no one can move
from his doorstep without going uphill,
unless it be to wade along the river. Four
principal roads and some lanes leave the
place, and by each of them there is an
ascent of two miles' length. Two miles uphill must be got over before rider or walker
reaches the summit, and then he is only
among the hills and has not surmounted
them. Some considerable part of the first
two miles on the slopes above the Exe is
cultivated. It is good land and yields well
though late, and has all been enclosed from
the moor.

One owner encloses a piece one year,
another the next; and thus Exmoor is
nibbled at. The circle slowly spreads, but
so slowly as to make no apparent impression; some fields, too, have fallen back
to rushes. When the first slope above
the Exe has been climbed, when the wayfarer has got out of the deep valley, he
comes at once to the moor, to heather
and whortleberry. There are sheep and
bullocks in the fields, but the whistle of
the curlew—true sign of the wilderness—
is heard among them. From the inhabited
places Exmoor is nibbled at, but is not
affected, any more than the drainage of fens
straitens the sea.

The boundless heather, which looks dark
in spring and early summer, at first sight
seems the only growth of the endless
moors. Among it, on closer examination,
will be found the light-green whortleberry

plants filling the spaces between, and in many districts there is a quantity of coarse grass. Every spring portions of the grass and heather are fired, and the flames travel with extraordinary rapidity, so that a mile seems traversed and the surface consumed almost immediately the match is applied. By waiting till the direction of the wind is suitable, the flames burn over the tract which has been selected, and are in a measure guided so as to avoid the districts which it is not desirable to destroy. Great fires like this again remind one of the prairies of America. After the fire the charred stems of furze alone remain, and gradually whiten and turn grey, like ribs of dead animals, in the winter. Among these crooked ribs the light-green whortle-berries and coarse grasses grow till they overtop the dry sticks. Next, the heather rises, and after a time the place resumes its

former aspect. Meanwhile, the new growth
of grass has afforded pasture to the sheep
and ponies, and to the deer.

Here and there small tufts of cotton on
stalks of grass appear waving in the breeze,
white dots above the dark heath. This
cotton-grass shows a boggy soil, and warns
the rider not to pass there lest his horse
sinks to the knee. Even in the hottest
summer months many places on the moors
—which, it must be remembered, are hill-
tops—retain water, and will let the unwary
sink. In winter these places are multiplied
tenfold, and it then needs a practised eye
to find a firm path between them. The turf
is much cut away for use as fuel ; it is
stacked, roots outwards, in heaps like hay-
cocks. This fuel has this advantage, that
the ashes have an agricultural value for
drilling in with turnips. But the holes
where it is removed become full of water,

which stays all the summer; they are, in fact, so many bogs, which horsemen should carefully avoid. Wild ducks are fond of these shallow ponds, for such they are— ponds thickly covered by green aquatic growths. On the higher slopes, where the heather has not been burned, it rises high, thick, and difficult to force a way through, so that the wayfarer must follow the paths made by the deer. Over these moors sheep, some bullocks, and ponies almost as wild as the deer, wander freely. Such is the North Forest, the centre of Red Deer Land — the home from which the red deer spread abroad. Though called the North Forest, it is bare of trees (except in the coombes); it is an open expanse of heather.

But the deer are no longer limited to the moors—they roam over a region of which Exmoor forms only a corner. With a pencil draw a line on the map from Bridgewater to near Ilfracombe, from Ilfracombe down to Exeter, and again from Exeter up to Bridgewater, enclosing a triangle, each side of which on the map would be about fifty miles, but to ride twenty more, on account of the irregular ground. It is not to be supposed that every acre of this region is visited by the deer, but either while wandering at their own will, or when running before the hounds, it is crossed and recrossed, and marked by their "slot," or footprints. You could not put your finger on any particular spot and say the herd is here, because their motions are so uncertain; one year they stay in one district, and the next go on to another.

They have been killed at the very gate of Exeter city, and recently Tiverton has become a pivot of the hunt. This country

contains a large part of Somerset and
Devon, Exmoor, and part of Dartmoor, the
Dunkery hills, and the steep Quantocks,
besides numerous minor ranges. The moors
of the Exe, the original home of the deer,
are but a corner. There are vast stretches
of fertile land in the valleys and plains,
cultivated to the highest degree, innumerable meadows, each with its thick hedges
and trees, so that with the copses and
covers they resemble woodlands. The triangle has within it not only moors and
hills, but good farming land, a city, and
many large towns. The paths of the deer
wind round about the rich and enclosed
districts, but if chased they frequently go
straight across them.

So wide a space may more aptly be
called a country than a district, and it is
strictly correct to say that the red deer are
not now local. They are the red deer of

the West of England, as wild and free as
in the days of Otterburn, when—

> " The dryvars thorowe the woodes went
>   For to reas the dear ;
> Bomen bickarte uppone the bent
>   With ther browd aras cleare."

II.

WILD EXMOOR.

THE long ascent, two miles of uphill road,
to the level of the moors, passes through
enclosed ground, where the deep valley
shelters the place from the winds of winter.
Thick hedges of beech run on either side
of the road in full June leaf, shutting out
all view and preventing the air from moderat-
ing the heat.　There is no current between

these hedges, which are not far apart, as the road is narrow, and the sense of heat is further increased by the slightly red tint of the dust. The hedges are ten feet high, and as much through, and beech grows close with well-leafed sprays, so that although the ascent is continuous, increasing elevation does not bring coolness. This impenetrability is of advantage to the cattle, sheltering them from storms and breaking the force of the tremendous gales which blow over Red Deer Land.

All the hedges beside the roads and about the fields are beech, for hawthorn will not grow to any height; the soil or the climate does not suit it, and it always remains thin and stunted. Beech springs up quickly and makes a very beautiful hedge to look at, especially in spring, when the leaf is in its first fresh green. These hedges grow above walls of loose stone, earth is banked against

the wall, and the beech flourishes upon it.
Long grass and moss droop over the stones
of the walls like arras, and are hollow beneath ; in these hollow spaces humble bees
have their nests. Ferns are almost as thick
as the grass, and sometimes where the walls
are exposed and without the arras of moss,
hart's-tongue springs from every crevice.
Foxgloves flower by the gateways, and from
every gateway there is a pleasant view of
the green valleys beneath, and of the dark
moors above.

At a distance the enclosed fields seem
surrounded with hedges, not merely cropped,
but smoothed and polished, so rounded and
regular do they appear. It is the natural
tendency of beech to grow to a regular
level, so that looking down upon it it appears cropped. I suppose the square shape
of most of the fields is caused by the walls ;
walls are more easily built in straight lines

than in curves. You see a spur of green hill—always much lower than the moors—surrounded at the summit by a square hedge (on a wall) like a square camp or forti-fication. This greater square is divided within into lesser squares. Without, fields, more or less square, descend the slope to the bottom of the valley, and each hedge, as just observed, is smooth, round, and of a polished green.

The road has the solid rock for founda-tion ; the rock sometimes comes to the sur-face, so that there is no dust or crumbled stone, and wheels run on the original hard ground. Approaching the summit the fields inside the beech hedge lose the green of those lower down, the grass is not so long and fresh, and is strewn with rushes. Pre-sently there is heather instead of sward, and the moor is on either hand. The road goes on over the hill, always between beech

hedges; but I left it here, and walked out
among the cotton-grass of the moor.

June had come in hot and dry, so that
the dark, peaty earth was firm, and com-
paratively easy to walk on. Even now there
were places where water stood, and I crossed
by stepping on thick tufts of matted grass,
dark water spirting aside under the pressure.
Where the turf had been cut away there
were ponds which it was necessary to go
round. Pale, short grass, the blades far
apart, and not close like the luxuriant growth
of a meadow, interspersed, too, with much
that was grey and dead, covered the broad
moor, which had been burnt in the spring.
My foot often caught in the dead stems of
furze withered by the flames. A lark rose
occasionally, else the expanse was vacant of
bird life—an immense distance only. There
was nothing but distance. How far was it
across this roll or undulation, how far was it

to the coombe yonder, how far to the range of hills beyond which rose higher than the high moors, then to the second range farther still, and to the third dim outline at the horizon?

These were the questions which continually arose. They were the only thoughts suggested by so much distance. The eye had nothing to rest on; it kept travelling farther, and whichever way I turned still there was the same space. It was twenty miles to the white cloud yonder looking through the air, and so it was twenty miles to the ridge, not the farthest, under it. The moor undulated on, now a coombe, now a rise, now pale grey-green where the surface had been burnt, and then dark where the heather was high; the moor undulated on, and it was twenty miles to the ridge and twenty to the cloud, and there was nothing between me and the cloud and the hill. A noise of thunder came, weary and travelling with difficulty. I glanced round; I could not see any cloud of thunderous character. How far could it have come? In enclosed countries thunder is not heard more than ten miles, but at this height—this seemingly level moor is twelve hundred feet above the sea—it may come how far?

Across from the Welsh mountains, over the Bristol Channel, up from the Devonshire tors, whence it is impossible to tell. I think the low boom reached me up the wind, but gazing under my hand for shade from the glare of the sun I cannot see any threatening vapour. There is only space, and sound perhaps may travel almost to infinity in space. The wind is cool, the sun fiery hot, the dry thin grass rustles under foot, and the dead furze stems, bleached by the weather, crack if stepped on. I wonder how far I have walked; the undulation whence I started has long disappeared behind another, and there is a third in front. I have crossed several boggy places, and passed many turf-ponds, and through acres of cotton-grass, waving like little white flags in the wind, and that is all; no hedges, no trees, no bushes even to mark progress by, not so much as a tall fern.

The low boom of thunder comes again out of the infinity of space, reminding me of the profundity around, but I will not look—I will not let my glance travel farther than what I judge must be half a mile or so ahead. By an effort I check it there, and will not look farther. I make an enclosure about me to shut out the vastness. In the shadowless open the sun's heat overpowers the wind, and renders movement laborious over the uneven ground. At last there is a hollow; it is the top, the shallow upper end of a coombe, which deepens as it descends into a valley. A spring rises

C

here, and by it there are a few short firs
and bushes, quite out of sight from the level
of the moor; for there are trees in the
hollows, but the glance of necessity passes
high over them.   Beyond the spring is a
wall; neither deer nor ponies heed it in the
least, and even the sheep can climb most of
the walls.   Within the wall I enter on the
heather, rising nearly to the knee, and tiring
to walk through, unless you follow paths or
select places less thickly covered.

The tips of the heather are fresh and
green, but the stems are dry and arid-look-
ing; they are wiry, hard, and unyielding.
Another distance, I do not know how far,
of dry dark heather continually fraying
against my knees, is traversed, when in front
appears a coombe, overgrown with heather
from summit to foot, and I stop suddenly.
On the opposite slope are five hinds lying
down, their heads visible above the heather,

"On the opposite slope are five hinds lying down,"—*Page* 34.

but too far for a good view. To stalk them it is necessary to go round the head, or shallow upper end of the coombe (a mile is nothing), and so get the wind to blow from them. Their scent is so quick that to approach down the wind is useless; they would scent me and be up and away long before I could get near. The hollow of the coombe carries the wind somewhat aslant just there from its general direction like a tube, else I think they would have scented me as it is.

As I start to go round the head of the coombe, suddenly some one whistles loudly, evidently as a signal to a friend, two loud notes; it is very annoying. The hinds will be off alarmed; I am surprised that they remain quiet; another whistle, and a bird, like a large peewit, but with pointed wings, crosses the coombe, rolling from side to side as it flies. It is a curlew — his whistle exactly resembled that of a man, but the deer were not deceived. On the moors curlew is locally pronounced almost without a vowel between the *c* and the *r*, and the *lew* as *loo—cr-loo*, the accent being on the last syllable. After a long detour, out of sight of the deer, I approached the coombe again from the opposite side, and found them presently. They had risen, and were feeding up the coombe, rather above me; I could see them cropping the green tips of the heather. They were rather of a brown than a red colour, their necks straight, and by the tail almost white. They fed in single file, and the wind coming from them, I crept up still nearer, almost within gunshot, till the leading hind, turning to pick at one side, saw me.

She viewed me intently a moment, and then jerked her head up, at which signal the other four lifted their heads with the same quick jerk and looked at me. The

leader lifted her head still higher, her ears
at a sharp angle, and in another moment
went off at a good pace, followed by the
rest. Hardly had they started, than three
more hinds appeared—they had been feeding lower in the coombe out of sight, and
raced after the five. Two of them were

"The whole eight paused in a group and watched me."

heavy in calf. So soon as they felt safe,
having got over a few hundred yards, the
whole eight paused in a group and watched
me. After a moment or two they trotted
again, again stopped and gazed at me; and
then taking no further notice, as I showed

no sign of pursuit, they began to graze, and so moved slowly on over the hill.

By the edge of the coombe I found their path; it was well trodden, and evidently much used; the heather was all bent down one way, leaning over downhill, but the dry stems and the hard ground had taken no impression or slot. In the dry heather the heat of the sun seemed greater than where the surface had been burnt, and walking was slow and difficult. But in a short time another coombe opened — the upper shallow end of a valley—and on the opposite side I saw a stag. He was lying down, but immediately got up, and looked straight across at me. His horns, in velvet, were not so high as his ears, but his coat was in perfect condition, a beautiful red gold colour, and he was a runnable deer, that is, of age and size sufficient for the chase. After a glance at me he turned, showing

the whiter colour of his tail, and went
quickly over the rising ground. As he started, a second male deer jumped
up from the heather, and followed him. This
was younger and smaller, and not nearly so
red—not much brighter in coat than a hind.
A runnable stag generally has a companion
like this with him. They were over the
hill quickly, and I followed; they had, however, disappeared when I reached the place.
A curlew whistled again, and suddenly three
heath-poults sprang up and flew hurriedly
away. Heath-poults, the female of black-
game, fly like a great partridge; they seem
to have the same curved wings, which appear
crescent-shaped as they go. These heavy
birds are as large as pheasants; the hen,
or heath-poult, is in general terms brown,
but it is a brown with buff under, crossed
in squares, or checks, a pattern very difficult to imitate.

Next I came to a coombe-head in which ran a streamlet, and at its sides were some small larches in their first green, pleasant to see among the dry dark heather. At this clear spring the deer often drink, and the cover—it is hardly a cover, for there are only a few trees—is a favourite spot with them to pass the day. There was no stag here in harbour at present; still, I stayed awhile by the splashing rivulet of water under the green larches between the rocky sides of the coombe. Out in the expanse of heather the open distances were oppressive; here in the hollow, with green to enclose the eye-glance, the solitude was a delight. The deer had been here quite recently, for there was fresh slot, or footmarks, both of stags and hinds, on a sandy path they used. All the coombes, the top or beginning of which I had passed, gradually deepen as the groove descends the

hill, till at the bottom they open upon a
wide valley at right angles, in which flows
the Badgeworthy Water. Each of these
rivulets goes to increase its stream, in
which full many a noble stag has come
to bay.

Over the valley rises a hill of red rock
thinly grown with oak—Badgeworthy Wood
—the green foliage of the oaks was faintly
yellow (spring yellow), and the red rock
showed between them. Dark heather, dark
and yet with some under-shade of purple,
covered the great slopes to the left of the
Wood. None of these colours, the yellow-
green of the oaks, the redness of the rocks,
the dark purple of the heather, were bright ;
they were toned and quiet, yet perfectly distinct in the brilliant sunshine. At the first
glance the colour was scarcely noticed ; in
a moment the eye became conscious of it,
and soon learned that to describe the scene

---

these tints must be alluded to. Gradually
the hues deepened as they were gazed at,
till the great hillside grew aglow with the
light they reflected.

All the view—the slopes, the wood, the
heather—was instinct with the presence of
the wild deer ; though sheltering in harbour from the heat, they were there. They
had passed under the green larches, which
were scarcely high enough to give me
shade—the sun at noon looked down between the trees—they had drunk from the
stream by the sallow, whose dark boughs
overhung it. I could have stayed and
dreamed there by the splashing water, but
there were yet more distances to be got
over. I climbed up the rocky side, and
from thence could see along the Badgeworthy Valley to the dull red precipice of
rocky fragments that overlooks the Lynn.
Passing more undulations of the moor there

opened another coombe, this time deep and
wide, and on the side towards me covered
by a thick growth of larches. On the
other it was bare.

As I followed a deer-path on the high
ground at the edge, but above the copse, I
continually saw marks of deer, slot of stag
and hind; some had been walking and
some galloping. Three blackcocks rose and
flew down the coombe, showing white streaks
among their black feathers; a bird, too,
like a cuckoo rose from the ground, and
flew to a little larch and perched on the
top. When I came nearer it flew on again,
and blundered into another larch; doubtless a goat-sucker, or fern-owl, clumsy by
day but swift at night. Suddenly two stags
broke cover out on the bare hillside opposite; they stopped and looked towards me.
It was a splendid sight, for they were so
near, within a stone's-throw, and being on

bare ground they were visible from slot to
brow. They were the same two I had seen
previously on the heather, but then further off.

On the ruddy golden coat of the warrantable deer the bright sunlight shone, so that
the colour seemed unsteady, or as if it was
visibly emanating and flowing forth in undulations. The same thing may be seen
about the white squares of rifle-targets under
the midsummer sun; though white, square,
and therefore by analogy well defined, there
is an unsteadiness of surface as if it came
a little towards you, and was wavy. The
deer are called red, and a few really appear
very red against the heather, but the greater
number of the stags are of a russet-gold,
and the hinds always more or less brown. I
do not know how to describe the stag's coat,
as he stood and looked at me, except by some
conjuncture of the colours red, or ruddy and

gold. Underneath the russet-red of the coat
there is a rich golden tint glowing through it.

Away he went the next minute, up the
steep coombe-side, and as he went, followed by his companion, the difference was
marked between their pace and that of the
hinds. Stags throw their forefeet out much
further, and hold their necks high, thrown
back; their going is so different, that by it
alone they can be distinguished at a distance from hinds. At the summit they
stayed again and regarded me, then moved
another quarter of a mile, and again looked
back; and so constantly stopping to watch
me, by degrees fetched a circle, and returned to the same cover far down in the
coombe. I have called these stags for the
convenience of writing, but strictly, in deer
language, the largest one old enough for
hunting was a stag; the other they would
now call a young male deer; in the olden

time he would have been called a brocke
or brocket.

As I turned from the fir-cover out into
the moor I noticed a small shrub of rhodo-
dendron flowering brightly among the dark
heather, far indeed from those tennis-lawns
with which it is associated about town.   It
was the only flower at that time in all the
miles of dark moor over which I had
walked under the burning sun.   Some one
had planted it, some one who loved the
tall deer.   If you can find it—*if*—you will
find a spot both wild and beautiful, for
there the distances are relieved by the
green firs of the coombe, and the oaks of
the wood across the valley.   But the boom
of thunder again rolling under an unclouded
sun once more reminded me of the im-
measurable horizon of Exmoor.

III.

DEER IN SUMMER.

A PATH leads along the edge of a round green hill standing by itself in the midst of the dark heather-covered moors which overlook it. In shape it resembles a skull-cap of green velvet imitated in sward, or it might be a great tennis-ball cut in two. This is Cloutsham Ball, and it looks like a green ball among the surrounding heather, contrasting in its colour and in its form with the moors. They undulate in long swelling contours; the Ball is globular. So round and smooth is the outline, that had it been carved with the chisel it could hardly have been more regular. From a distance it appears much smaller than it is, a mere

D

toy at the foot of the vast moors, but it is a mathematical fact that the spheroid form concentrates more substance in a given measurement than any other.

Afar, too, the glance naturally rests on the top, and does not observe the enlargement of the base. The illusion is increased by the division of the summit into four fields by a wall in the shape of a Maltese cross. Four meadows are nothing in the midst of the expanse to which one is accustomed on the hills, but in reality the base of the Ball is a very long way round. There are projecting stones for steps in the wall on the summit, by which it can be climbed, and the path followed along the edge of the Ball. The sward is hard to the footsteps, for it does but cover the rock beneath; there is grass, but no turf. Brake fern grows towards the verge, and bushes and brambles fringe it. Putting the foot carelessly on a bunch of grass, the loose stones it conceals slip, and it is necessary to quickly grasp a stout stem of fern to avoid a fall.

Reddish stones lie by the bushes, some on the surface, and others partly embedded in the ground. Red stones are everywhere under the grass; some of them roll at a touch. Looking down the descent increases in steepness, for the trunks of the oaks beneath are almost parallel with the side of the hill. It is possible to get down, but the loose stones would render it awkward, and even dangerous in places to those unused to such footing. The deer go up and down, and pass along the steepest parts easily, entering the meads on the summit where the grass is fresh and sweet, for they will always have the best of everything. They have their own especial tracks across and aslant the Ball; the thin grass and hard red stones do not show much impression, still their paths can be traced by the worn sward and by the hollow their hoofs work in the stones like a shallow furrow.

A hawthorn bush in bloom has the ends of many of its boughs cut off as if with a knife. This was done by the deer in early spring, when the first green leaves came forth, sappy and sweet, and were eagerly nibbled. I cannot look round while picking a way over this grassy and yet rugged ground without risk of stumbling, but on pausing a moment the shape of the place is evident. Across a deep valley—a rifle-shot distant — rises a steep slope covered with oak. Openings in the oaks are green with brake, and where the fern has not grown the reddish hue of the loose stones is visible. The slope is far higher than the hill on which I stand, and extends right and left, surrounding me. To the left it

is all woods! woods! woods!—a valley of
woods, interminable oak, under which hundreds of deer might hide. On the right
it is heather—thousands of acres of heather
—gradually expanding into the mountainous
breadth of Dunkery Beacon.

Now in June the heather is dark, yet beneath the darkness there are faint shades of
purple and green ; it looks dry and heated
under the sunshine. Dunkery towers over
as if the green Ball were a molehill. I
can see now that a deep trench—a natural
fosse--surrounds me on every side, except
where a neck of land like a drawbridge
gives access to the mount. Go in what
direction you will, you are met by this
immense circular trench, and beyond that
by a steep and high ascent. The heather
and the woods of the opposite slopes wind
round you, so that by merely crossing the
summit of the mount you change one view

over miles of heather for another over miles
of wood.

It is a great natural stage erected in the
centre of a circular theatre of moor and
forest, and the spectator has only to face in
different directions to watch the hunt travel
round him. While the hunt has to go miles,
he has but to stroll a few hundred yards;
presently the deer, breaking cover, comes
up over the summit of the Ball by one of
its scarcely visible paths, and crosses it in
front of him within a stone's-throw. If an
army had cast up a rocky stand for a Xerxes
to view the sport, they could not have done
it more effectually.

I divide the broad heather slope opposite
into sections mentally, so as to be able to
search it thoroughly for deer. Merely to
glance at so wide an expanse would be useless; the only way is to examine it piece
by piece from the summit to the valley, as

if it were marked in lines like a map. From a spot where the heather is thin and the red stones show, to a bush, is one division; between a rough track and a hollow is another; there is then a slight change in the colour of the surface, sufficient to form a resting-place for the eye, and beyond that some mountain sheep are settled. I look slowly down each of these parallels, commencing at the summit and letting the eye gradually descend, so that the vision does not miss the least portion. Every acre is thus examined, and nothing could be missed. Some sheep on the ridge for a moment attract attention; either there is a slight vapour there, or it is an effect of mirage, for they appear larger than sheep, but their motions are not those of deer. Neither stag nor hind is feeding nor lying down in the heather.

The oak woods cannot be so scrutinised;

their shadowy masses are impenetrable, and all that can be done is to look into each opening where fern occupies the space between the trees. Under the oak boughs and in the thickets the stags can lie perfectly unseen ; and the brake, too, is high enough to hide them if lying down. In June the deer spend the whole of the day in the covers out of the heat. At this time they are more shy than at any other, both stags and hinds retiring out of sight. The stags' antlers are as yet only partially grown, and while these weapons are soft and tender they conceal themselves. The hinds have their calves only recently dropped, or are about to calve, and consequently keep in the thickest woods.

One might walk across the entire width of the North Forest, and not see a single deer, and yet be in the midst of them ; and so it is common for fishermen to whip for

trout day after day for weeks together along
streams which wind through favourite covers
without obtaining a glimpse of deer.   Wild

Cloutsham
Ford

and shy, they are lost in the foliage of
their woods, and are only to be found with
much labour and in certain particular places.

At Cloutsham occasionally they may be observed lying among the heather opposite, those deer that keep to the hill being less regular in retiring to the woods than the rest. A stag, too, sometimes comes out from his harbour, and may be viewed under the oaks.

There are none visible to-day on this side of the Ball, so I walk round the mount, passing a very large mountain-ash in flower; a branch has been broken from it, but it is still a fine tree. The mountain-ash grows freely on the hillsides wherever a tree can take root. A sound which I thought I heard just now rises and becomes distinctly audible; it is the rush of swift water, and comes up through the oaks from the hollow of the giant fosse. The name of the stream is Horner Water, flowing by Horner Wood along the bottom of the deep trench. A wind draws across the summit of the Ball, bending the brake stems and stirring the

mountain-ash. It is pleasant in the shade
to feel the cool air and listen to the water
far below.

Is that a spot of red yonder in an opening
between the oaks—is it a stag? Colour it
is of some kind against the fern, but my
eyes have become so weary with intently
gazing that I think they would recognise
any hue as the red for which they are looking. After resting them a few moments on
the brake and grass at my feet, I look again,
and see at once that it is a piece of faded
furze; the yellow bloom is going, and it
was this that deceived me. No apparent
connection exists between red and yellow;
it proves how weary the visual nerves must
be when they can only determine that it is
colour, and cannct distinguish hues. I have
been gazing intently for an hour, scarcely
closing the lids, and under the bright light
of a summer noon. It is not just glancing

across, but the careful mapping of every acre
that has strained them. Merely looking for
a few moments downwards at the grass
under foot completely restored the power of
distinguishing colour.

I went on further, and stayed again to
examine a reddish spot; this time it was
where a path could be seen for a yard or
two under the oaks. A third time a fragment of rock held the glance for a second
or two; no, that is not the shape nor the
tint wished for. These great woods will
disappoint me; I shall not see any deer,
but I will go down and walk, or rather
climb, through them somehow. Suddenly,
as I looked once more, I caught sight of a
red mark in the midst of an acre of brake
surrounded by oak. I was sure it was a
stag instantly by the bright colour, by the
position, and yet if questioned I could not
have positively asserted that I had any

reason for my opinion at all. Certainty
does not always depend upon proofs that
can be explained. A secret judgment exists
in the mind and acts on perceptions too
delicate to be registered. I was certain it
was a stag, and the glass at once confirmed
my eyes.

He was standing in the fern beside a bush,
with his head down as if feeding. The great
oak woods were about him, above and below,
and the sunlight fell on the golden red of
his coat. A whistle—the sound was a moment or two reaching him—made him lift
his head, and the upright carriage of the
neck proved again that it was a stag and
not a hind. His antlers had not yet risen
as high as his ears. Another whistle—he
lifted his head yet higher but did not move,
for he knew he was safe. The whistle
sounded to him faint across the hollow
space, and his keen eyes and still keener

nostrils assured him that there was no
danger. I wished to see him closer, and
went down a path which descends the side
of the green mount.

The path is a groove worn in loose and
sliding stones, steep and slippery because
the stones give way, yet it is down this
that the huntsman rides and those who
follow him. I found it awkward enough
on foot till under the oaks lower down,
where there were fewer loose red stones.
Here the sound of rushing water grew much
louder, and in a minute or two the stream
appeared, running at a great speed over the
rocky fragments of its bed. Across this
beautiful stream a tree had been thrown
and hewn flat at the upper side; this, with
a hand-rail, formed a bridge for foot pas-
sengers. Upon the opposite side a track
went beside the water through the woods.
Stalking silently along the path, I came

presently under the stag, and watched him from behind a tree; he was so near that his slightest motion was visible.

He stood breast-deep in brake, and there was a purple foxglove in flower just beside him. There seemed the least possible fleck of white among the golden russet of his side. After I had looked long enough, a shout sent him with one bound into the thicket; and although the boughs did not appear very close together, he was immediately hidden. He moved easily along the steep slope where even hounds sometimes find a difficulty in following.

Some distance further I found another foot-bridge made of a smoothed tree, and sat down upon it at the verge of the brook. Insects had emerged from the timber, leaving their cases stretching forth from the mouths of their drilled holes. The timber was furrowed and gouged by the mandibles of wasps, who had carried the wood away for the paper of their nests. Ferns on the bank, and confervæ on the rocky fragments, gave the stream a green tint; the reflection of the oak boughs over did not form a clear image, but was drawn along by the irregular motion, forming a green surface. Red rocks beneath the water, and dark places where it was deeper, added a brown hue. The beautiful brook ran strong and swift in all the vigour of youth, caring nothing for the stones over which it leaped. By its side oak-trees stood; the glance passed for a long way between the trunks, and the ground was thickly grown with fern and foxglove. The hillside in places overhung, and large roots descended like pillars to support it.

On either hand the steep slopes of the valley were wooded to the top, and yonder the round green summit of the Ball ap-

"The deer rush to the swift brook."—*Page* 67.

peared above the trees. The height could
be estimated by the diminution in the apparent size of the oaks. At such a stream
Rosalind might have slaked her thirst and
found her name carved close by in the soft
bark of a mountain-ash; it is a spot where
the influence of Shakespeare is unconsciously felt. The interest the scene itself
arouses is so much increased by the presence of the deer, for though unseen in
the summer noon, they are certainly here
as wild as ever they were in fair Rosalind's time. This is their favourite stream;
they come down to it to drink at mid-
day, and return to the cover to wait till
night.

When the tufters enter the woods—that
is, the hounds detached from the pack to
force the deer to break cover—the deer rush
to the swift brook, aware that it leaves no
scent. To and fro the stream they race,

and in their terror will often pass under people standing on the foot-bridge. Till absolutely compelled they will not leave the water ; they will return to it again and again a little lower down, and are only driven from it with continued chasing. Frequently, if roused far away on the open moors of the North Forest, they will make at once straight for Horner Water. Then again, after a long run, when they feel their strength ebbing, they will circle back to die in their beloved stream. There is a projecting rock by the brook, standing out from the hillside, to which a stag once retreated, and, with his back to the precipice, kept the hounds at bay. It was the same as if he had been at the end of a steep wall, and he would never have been driven from his position by the hounds unaided by man. Stags will often do this when they can no longer keep in front of the pack.

A high projecting rock, or a narrow path
that will only permit the hounds to approach
them in one direction, is a fortress. A stag
can face the hounds and defend himself
with his terrible brow-points so long as
they are obliged to meet him. But he
knows he cannot fight successfully if as-
sailed from all sides; baffled by so many,
he is ultimately pulled down. So the stag
chooses an isolated rock, or a narrow footpath, as at Glenthorne, with inaccessible
rocky walls above and beneath, and then
turns on his pursuers. As he runs he
thinks, and reviews in his mind the various
places he has visited previously. His course
is not determined by accident but by fore-
thought. He sees the river in his mind,
the river at which he has so often quenched
his thirst, and fleetly travels towards it.
He remembers the rock, or the precipitous
footpath, and hastens thither. He thinks

of a pond, and takes it in his way to cool himself by a plunge.

Horner Wood is so large and difficult that there is always much trouble in getting the deer to quit it. Sometimes the hounds divide, and follow two. A hind thus pursued by a few hounds and hard pressed, threw them off by crossing the stream, and took refuge in the fern high up the hill. But she had been observed by a runner; he called the hounds, and with the greatest difficulty climbed up over the loose stones. He put them right on her; she sprang from the spot, overthrowing him in her wild haste, but the hounds had the scent, and she was taken. Sometimes a stag will not leave Horner Water at all. On being roused he goes to the stream and runs down it for miles, out from the woodlands, through the cultivated plain, right to the shore of the Channel, and then to sea, never quit-

ting the water from the first start to his
death.

Where the woods cease and the coombe
opens stands Horner Mill, which has a

large iron overshot wheel exposed at the side of the building. Deer running down the stream usually break from it as they come to the hatch just above the mill-wheel, and go round the mill, which blocks their course along the brook. Once a hind closely followed was so beset by the hounds that, unable to quit the brook, she leaped from the sluice on to the top of the revolving wheel. The immense iron wheel carried her over and threw her to the ground, disabling her. She was immediately killed to prevent suffering. Marks of the passage of a traction-engine may be seen in the road to the mill; it is used to draw loads to and from the place, and comes to the edge of the haunts of the deer—the most modern of machines beside the ancient chase.

Returning to the Ball, the path up it over the loose stones seems yet steeper than when descending. On the summit it now goes among oaks standing wide apart; through these, deer sometimes run, one of their tracks leading up here and over the mount. Cloutsham Farm stands where the neck of

Cloutsham
Farm

land connects the round green mount with the general level of the moors. The old thatched house—it is one of Sir Thomas Acland's thatched houses—has a hearth as wide as that of a hunting lodge should be, and an arched inner doorway of oak. A rude massiveness characterises the place. A balcony on the first floor overlooks the steepest part of the vast natural fosse surrounding the mount, and the mountainous breadth of Dunkery Beacon rises exactly opposite, shutting out the lower half of the sky.

Something is now moving among the heather near the summit, so distant and so dim that it is difficult to distinguish what it is. But the sheep yonder are white and these three animals are dark, a little inclined to redness. They move quickly in line, and are larger than sheep; they must be hinds. It is only when endeavouring to determine what any particular object is, that you recognise the breadth and height of the Beacon side. It is much farther and much higher than the eye at first acknowledges.

A level yet elevated spot called Sweetre, or
Sweet Tree, at the foot of Dunkery, where
there is some sward and furze, is much fre-
quented by deer. For years they haunted
it ; they still do so, but not so much now,
for they change from place to place according to their wild caprice.

IV.

ANTLER AND FERN.

THE green stem of the brake fern as it rises
unrolls at the top, and when these coils
appear in the spring the stag's new horns
begin to grow. Fern and antler start together; the fern is easily found, for it is
soon taller than the thin grass, but the
stag conceals himself in the cover, and it
is not easy to know to what stage he has
arrived. But his new antlers grow with
the fern, and as that reaches a good height
so his horns begin to overtop his ears.
Brake is later on the moors than in the
warm southern counties; for although Exmoor is in the same latitude, it is so exposed
that grass and flower are behind the time

usual elsewhere. Brake, however, grows
rapidly when it once rises out of the bare
ground at the sides of the coombes, or between the oaks of the covers, and soon has
knots, or rather branches—where, if cut
across, the figure of an oak-tree appears.
When the heated August atmosphere has
begun to tint the fern in southern counties
with a faint yellow, stag-hunting commences.

The deer are fond of the fern to hide in,
and they sometimes take a little of the tips
of the fronds. Immense quantities of fern
are cut and carried away, both on the moors
and the Quantock Hills—which are moors
too—for use as litter. All the deer country
is full of ferns—on the slopes, in the woods,
the hedgerows, the walls, and the sides
of old buildings—from the tree-like brake
down to the little wall-rue, they flourish
luxuriantly. The hinds seek the cover of
the ferns when their calves are born, and

there hide them; and the little creatures lie through the heat of the summer day among it. Fawn has a pleasanter sound than calf, but by all the rules of venery, ancient and modern, the young of the fallow deer are fawns, those of the tall red deer are called calves. Upon the moors the ferns grow principally towards coombes and covers, more so than among the heather; and these coombes, with water and shade, are the favourite haunts of the deer.

Every wall they climb over is covered with fern in summer. These walls are made of loose flat stones, between the joints of which the pennywort leaves come forth and send up a stalk to bear the flowers—the leaves are round like green pennies. Though less conspicuous the pennyworts are almost as numerous as the ferns, and the two are often crushed under the deer's hoofs, or slot. It is the hinds who climb the walls; the stags

leap to the top, which is always broad, and
then down the other side. Hinds get their
forefeet — it is inconvenient to write slot
always—on the top of the wall, and their
hind hoofs dig into the earth and loose
stone, making a sort of step.

They soon open a gap in the hedge on
the top of the wall by going through so
often, night after night, always at the same
spot, and the step becomes well marked.
By this step in the wall the calf climbs up,
and follows his mother; he could not spring
on to the top at once, and the hinds choose
the best places they can for their young to
get over. The pennyworts are crushed, the
fern broken down, and the red sand of the
bank dug out; while on the top a gap—
called a rack—is formed through the beech
hedge. By these racks the hinds and calves
pass from the moors into the cultivated
fields. Near the covers and coombes where

the fern is thick the deer-paths are distinct. In hind-hunting time the brake is bronzed, or brown from frost; it holds the dew, or the thawed rime of the winter nights, and soaks those who attempt to walk among it. As it rises again in spring it helps to hide the dropped antlers of the stag.

The antlers fall in March; though so hard and capable of giving a wound like a spear, they are not fixed to the bone of the head, nor do they grow like the cow's horn — deeply rooted; they seem, indeed, to have scarcely any root or hold, and yet are perfectly firm till the proper time arrives to shed them. The stag then retires into the woods, and, it is believed, tries to drop his horns in a place where he thinks they are least likely to be found. He separates himself from his companion stags, and keeps alone at this moment. It is possible that he may drag brambles or branches over the dropped antlers if they chance to grow at hand; for it is remarkable that few horns are found compared to the number that must be shed, and those that are found are more often single horns than pairs. Certainly the extent of the woods is very great, but they are traversed by gamekeepers and others, the moors are crossed by shepherds, and all keep a keen look-out for horns which are valuable.

A good pair will fetch £5; as much as £10 has been given for a pair with a remarkable number of points. These prices alone show that it is not so easy to find a pair of dropped antlers as might be imagined. A gamekeeper, in one wood, one season found eight horns running, all single, that is, belonging to one side of the head only. Many of the horns sold are really odd antlers, and were dropped by different stags; these are fitted together, and gene-

F

rally to a hind's head. The stag's head is the property of the Master of the Stag-hounds, and it is taken possession of for him when a stag is killed ; consequently few genuine heads of the red stag come into the market.

To all but a "forester good," a hind's head looks as natural as a stag's when fitted with horns, and fastened to the wall. A single horn will bring a sovereign, and it is by collecting these single horns that most of the pairs are formed, excluding, of course, those presented by the Master. Few pairs thus put together are good, and some very inferior. Somehow or other the stags, and those that bear good heads especially, have a way of dropping their antlers in the most unlikely places. Leaves that have fallen from the beech-trees and hedges are blown along by the spring gales and cover them, dead ferns droop over, and their colour is but little different from the grey grass and dead branches. Or the heather conceals the horn, and it is possible to walk right over it without seeing it.

An ardent forester who was racing on foot after the hounds, the pack being in full cry, caught his foot in descending a coombe-side, and rolled some distance. He supposed it was a furze stem, or a tree root, but on rising he chanced to look at his foot, and found it firmly fixed in a stag's antler. He had trod, as he ran, right between the two points on top, which threw him like a trap, and over he went, carrying the horn with him in his descent. So well had the antler been concealed by the heather that he had not seen it, and would not have known of its existence had he not stepped on it. It seems as if the antlers were more often found by chance than when carefully looked for, which has given rise to the idea that the stag anticipates intelligent search, and hides accordingly.

An antler is judged by the number of points or tines which spring from the beam. The beam is the main stem, and the points are the branches. The beam itself varies much, and is valued according to its round- ness and thickness. Some are very thick, and others spindly, like a tree that has been drawn up beyond its strength in a plantation. Close to the head a point springs from the beam and is curved up- wards : this is called the brow-point. Just over it a second starts, in shape resembling the first, but not so long or large : this is called the bay. These two are close together, and defend the brow of the stag. There is then an interval, till some way up the beam, or main· stem, a third—the tray—appears. At the upper end the antler divides into three points, called three on top. This is a full horn ; brow, bay, tray, and three on top, or six points a side for each antler—twelve for the pair. Sometimes there are additional points starting from the beam like the tray, but not so long, making thirteen, or more, points to the antlers. Besides these, little knobs appear on the beam like points about to grow, which are said to be " offers," as if a point had offered to grow there.

In reckoning an antler with these they say twelve points (or more, as the case may be) and an offer. Twelve is sometimes exceeded, as many as fifteen, and even in one case twenty points and offers having been known. Not all the antlers reach twelve, generally failing in the top-points. Often there are only two on the top instead of three, and sometimes the top of the antler is not divided and only gives one point. Occasionally the absence of the top points is the result of malformation, but is

usually a sign that the stag had not reached
maturity.

The length and thickness of the beam or
stem, the number of points and offers of
points, and the width between the tips of
the horns as they grow on the head are all
reckoned in estimating antlers. Such are
the terms commonly used in the present day
on Exmoor ; but in ancient times connois-
seurs of the chase had numerous others, such
as the burr, the pearls, the gutters, royals,
and sur-royals. Crowned heads and forked
heads, however, are still spoken of when the
antler forks, or when the points draw together in the outline of a crown.

The ancient terms began with the " burr ; "
this was the thickened base of the horn (or
beam) where it joins the head. It is there
enlarged and rough like the base of an oak-
tree at the ground. " Burr," as a term ex-
pressive of bulging, is still in use by black-

smiths, who speak of raising a "burr" on a
rivet by hammering it—the "burr" is the
bulging caused by the blows. Above the
"burr" came the brow-antlier, now the
brow-point; next the bez-antlier, now the
bay (bez doubtless was pronounced bay).
The third point, now called the tray—French
trés, hunting terms are derived from Norman-French—was then the royal, and the
top-points or crown was the sur-royal-top.
The gutters were the seams or grooves in
the main stem or beam; the pearls appear
to have been the little knobs about the
"burr." Sometimes the brow-point was
called simply the antlier, and the bay the
sur-antlier, and the top the croche. There
was a complete science of reckoning an
antlier; the meaning of some of the terms
seems to have varied with the number of
points, and there were many other minutiæ.
Those now in use on Exmoor are distinct

enough, and are given above as plainly as possible.

It is characteristic of the English red deer that the brow-points are always longer than the bay-points, those next to them. Indian deer have the bay-points longer than the brow—exactly the reverse. A pair of Indian antlers are fixed in the huntsman's porch at Exford, and beside these he has a pair of Exmoor horns, which he succeeded in getting hold of, and which resemble the Indian in this particular. For once the Exmoor horns have the second points longest—the exception demonstrating the rule.

As the new horns grow on the stag's head they are at first soft and even flexible, and the stag is careful to avoid striking them against anything. They are covered with a skin called the velvet; it is of a brown colour, soft, like plush. While this bark or skin remains on the horn the stag is said to

be in velvet and is not hunted. Towards
the end of July, as the horns become hard,
the skin is supposed to tickle and irritate,
and the stag rubs his head against trees to
get rid of it. By degrees it peels off, and
he is then in a fit condition for the chase.
One or two of the first stags killed generally
have remnants of the velvet adhering to the
horns, hanging in strips as they run. Fragments of velvet are snatched up as trophies
by those in at the death ; but after the first
week the velvet has entirely gone, and no
more are killed with it.

A stag at bay is not to be approached
without great caution, for with his antlers
he can inflict formidable wounds. Hounds
are sometimes killed, and frequently injured.
The part of the antler with which most
mischief is done is the brow-point. This
starts from the brow near the head and
curves upwards, and when the stag holds

his head low, as he does in delivering a
blow, the sharp end of the brow-point pro-
jects almost straight in front of him. The
two brow-points, one on each side, at that
moment resemble the points of a hay-fork,
or prong—called on Exmoor a pick—and
if he can catch a hound on either of the
tips he is certain to leave a terrible mark.
If he can get the hound between him and
a rock, or a stone or a bank, so as to have
something firm to push against, the brow-
point will transfix the hound like a spear.

These points indeed are sometimes called
spears. They are not so conspicuous as the
upper part of the antler, which would naturally be supposed the most dangerous ; but
it is from these that wounds are generally
received. The tips are not sharp in the sense
that a dagger-point is said to be sharp ; they
are bluntly sharp, sufficiently so to penetrate
easily when driven with the tremendous force

of the stag's muscular neck. So long as he can face the hounds with these, with rocks at his side, or a precipice, so that they can only run in in front, he can defy them. Now and then it happens during a long run that the main part of the pack is distanced by one or two swift hounds. They leave the pack behind and pursue unsupported. When a stag becomes aware of this he will sometimes turn and face them in his path, knowing that he can deal with them.

One day a fine hound in advance like this was suddenly confronted by the stag, who, with a blow of the formidable brow-point, ripped the hound open so that his entrails touched the ground. The huntsman, coming up, dismounted, and with his usual presence of mind replaced the intestines ·in the gaping wound ; by good fortune they were not broken. He had no thread or needle, and could not get any to sew up the wound, but he managed to fasten it together with pins. In this condition the hound was carried home, and the wound properly sewn up. He recovered quickly, and in a very short time was running again with the pack as if nothing had occurred. A similar accident happened to another hound; only, in this case a house being near, a needle and thread were procured, and the wound sewn at once. This hound, too, got well, and was running about in a fortnight. The good condition in which the hounds are kept no doubt had much to do with this rapid healing.

Instances are not uncommon of men getting a blow from the antlers when a stag is at bay. If he is not thoroughly exhausted he will jerk his antlers viciously at any one who comes near, and many have received wounds by going in carelessly. The huntsman himself once had a knock in the face;

the horn struck the left side of the nose
and ripped the skin off, fortunately doing no
further injury. The wound healed perfectly,
and gave no trouble ; he has never found it
necessary to use anything more than a little
Friar's Balsam for such hurts, and has never
known any harm come of them. There is
an ancient belief that hart's horns are poisonous, and that wounds inflicted by them
are difficult to heal. Much may depend
upon the position of a wound, and also on
the state of health of the person injured,
but certainly experience with the Exmoor
harts is in favour of the horn not being
poisonous.

The whipper-in carries a waterproof bag,
and when the stag is killed the horns and
head are placed in it to preserve them from
disfigurement by blood or dirt. Sometimes
one antler has four points on the top, and
the other only three ; sometimes the top is

hollow and will hold a glass of wine. Pipe-
bowls are made of the butt-end of the beam.
Besides being his weapons of offence the
horns to some extent are the stag's armour.
As he starts he throws his head well back,
and the horns fit each side of his neck or
shoulder, and so guard him from the thick
thorn bushes into which he often plunges.
Young hounds sometimes seize the antler,
but quickly leave hold. The new horns, as
before observed, begin to grow with the
brake fern, and the velvet is rubbed off
towards the end of July, or beginning of
August, so that they take four months to
come to this complete state. At the same
time the hart or stag sheds his coat, and
in June appears in his full red-gold colour.

In October again, as the stag-hunting
ceases, the horns are employed in fighting,
the stags then combating for their lady-loves.
The life of a stag is indeed so bound up

with the growth and condition of his antlers
that it may be said to begin and end with
them. Before they are high enough to be
dignified as horns the young male deer runs
with the hinds and herds with them. There
is little difference in their appearance, and
it sometimes happens in the hind-hunting
season that a young male deer is chased
for some time till the mistake is discovered.
The outline of the face is broader and
shorter—a hind's face looks longer—and by
this the heads may be distinguished. As
he grows older, and the antlers each season
become larger, the deer leaves the hinds
and joins the stags, feeding and harbouring
in company with one of them. At last a
full-grown stag, he is in his turn master,
and has a companion, as it were, to fag
for him. In his old age the antlers each
year diminish in points and size, the beam
becomes thinner, and from four on top the

points dwindle to three, and then to two,
so as to look like those of a young stag.

There is no more beautiful creature than
a stag in his pride of antler, his coat of
ruddy gold, his grace of form and motion.
He seems the natural owner of the ferny
coombes, the oak woods, the broad slopes of
heather. They belong to him, and he steps
upon the sward in lordly mastership. The
land is his, and the hills, the sweet streams,
and rocky glens. He is infinitely more
natural than the cattle and sheep that have
strayed into his domains. For some inexplicable reason, although they too are in
reality natural, when he is present they look
as if they had been put there and were kept
there by artificial means. They do not, as
painters say, shade in with the colours and
shape of the landscape. He is as natural
as an oak, or a fern, or a rock itself. He is
earth-born—autochthon—and holds posses-

"Proud as a Spanish noble."—*Page* 99.

G

sion by descent. Utterly scorning control,
the walls and hedges are nothing to him—
he roams where he chooses, as fancy leads,
and gathers the food that pleases him.

Pillaging the crops and claiming his dues
from the orchards and gardens, he exercises
his ancient feudal rights, indifferent to the
laws of house-people. Disturb him in his
wild stronghold of oak wood or heather, and,
as he yields to force, still he stops and looks
back proudly. He is slain, but never conquered. He will not cross with the tame
park deer; proud as a Spanish noble, he dis-
dains the fallow deer, and breeds only with
his own race. But it is chiefly because of
his singular adaptation and fitness to the
places where he is found that he obtains
our sympathy.

The branching antlers accord so well with
the deep shadowy boughs and the broad
fronds of the brake; the golden red of his

coat fits to the foxglove, the purple heather,
and later on to the orange and red of the
beech; his easy bounding motion springs
from the elastic sward; his limbs climb the
steep hill as if it were level; his speed
covers the distances, and he goes from
place to place as the wind. He not only
lives in the wild, wild woods and moors—
he grows out of them, as the oak grows
from the ground. The noble stag in his
pride of antler is lord and monarch of all
the creatures left to us in English forests
and on English hills.

V.

WAYS OF RED DEER.

A STAG used to be called a "forester" in the days when stag-hunting had fallen to a low estate, and every one shot or poached the wild deer as they chose. With so many guns against them all over Exmoor and the neighbouring districts, the red deer grew scarce, and were not often seen. They were, in fact, in some danger of extinction, being treated as outlaws and killed in and out of season. If any one sighted a stag, or found the slot, he roused the country-side; people armed themselves with guns of every kind and sallied forth to destroy it. If a stag was shot, he was put into a cart and carried through the place in triumph. Poachers followed the deer continually, and thinned their numbers.

It happened once that a "forester" was discovered in a certain district, and a party was quickly formed to go out and shoot the stag. Among those who went was a man well known as a successful deer-shot, upon whose good aim they chiefly relied. They took with them a gallon of spirits. After some time spent in searching for the stag, and just as they were beginning to weary of the attempt, up the "forester" jumped close to the party. A volley was fired—the muzzles almost touching the stag —but the game went off at full speed. The old gunner, however, declared that he had hit the mark; he was sure he had aimed straight. In a minute or two, as they watched the stag bounding up the hill a mile away, suddenly he dropped and lay still, evidently dead. It was found afterwards that the ball from the old gunner's weapon had grazed the stag's heart, and yet with that wound he had run upwards of a mile. No other bullet had struck him ; it was a wonder where all the balls had gone to, for the shooters were so close to each other they narrowly escaped wounding themselves by the cross fire.

The party were so tired of walking after the stag that they did not go at once to ascertain if he was really dead, or to cut the throat. They sat down in the heather to refresh themselves with the spirits, and so well did they do this that by-and-by the old gunner fell firm asleep. Neither blows nor shouts could rouse him, so in order to wake him up they set fire to the heather, little thinking of what they were doing. Dry as tinder, the heather blazed up in such a fury of flame that they fled aside to get out of the way, leaving the sleeper to his fate.

The flame passed over him as he lay, and when the wind had driven it along they found him in his burning clothes. They could not put the burning clothes out, and so carried him to the river and dipped him in. He was terribly scorched and half drowned, and was long ill, but ultimately recovered. Though the heather burnt with such ferocity the flame was quick, almost like a flash of gunpowder, and was gone over in a moment; still it was a very narrow escape from a dreadful death. The thing was done in a frolic, but such frolics are very dangerous. Many acres of heather were burned, and considerable pecuniary damage caused.

Now, it is the rarest thing to hear of a stag being shot, or of any deer-poaching, though the deer are so numerous and could often be easily killed. They certainly were shot from time to time later than the date

of the above anecdote, generally by small
farmers into whose fields they had strayed
and committed serious damage. A farmer
who had shot a deer put the animal as
soon as possible into the salter out of sight.
There are people here and there still to be
found who have eaten poached venison, but
there is not one now to be found who will
confess to having shot a deer. So greatly
has popular opinion changed during the last
seven-and-twenty years on Exmoor that at
the present day were a man to shoot a stag
he would be utterly sent to Coventry. No
one would speak or deal with him or acknowledge his existence. He would be
utterly cut off from society of every class,
not only the upper but the lower classes
being equally imbued with the sporting
feeling.

Nor, indeed, is there any possibility of
poaching. A stag is a large animal which

cannot be put in a pocket like a hare, nor cooked and eaten at once. The skin and antlers, slot and head, are not to be easily destroyed. No one would buy a stolen deer, knowing the inevitable consequences; and as there are no receivers—as there are of poached pheasants—there are no thieves. Even the labouring classes have not the least desire to destroy them; on the contrary, they know full well that the stag-hunting is profitable to them, causing, as it does, so much money to circulate in innumerable ways. Without stag-hunting there would be absolutely nothing doing about Exmoor—no life, no movement—so that it proves of the greatest value to all. The cottager, as well as the sportsman, drinks the toast inscribed on the silver buttons worn on the scarlet coats of the hunt, " Prosperity to Stag-Hunting."

Poaching, however, did not quite die out

for some years, and if they were not very
good shots, still if the deer was but wounded
they would follow him up for days till they
got him. Some twelve years since a man
returned from the gold-diggings, and who
seems to have been an adventurous, not to
say desperate character, shot a stag, one out
of three lying in some heather not far from
his home. The horns till lately hung in the
cottage. The fact soon came to the knowledge of the harbourer, who hunted him, as
it were, by slot, till at last he captured
him, with the assistance of a police-constable,
in the highway. In his pockets they found a
gun taken to pieces for convenience of con-
cealment, a revolver, and a long bowie-knife.

This appears to have been the last case
of deliberate deer-stealing. If any have
occurred since, it has been rather casually
than by deliberate pursuit. Deer wandering
into fields held by small farmers have, it is

believed, been shot, but even this practice
has quite died out. At this hour a red stag
is perfectly safe from one side of Exmoor
to the other, no matter whether he may be
in the oak covers, on the heather, or eating
his fill in the wheat-fields. Of William the
Conqueror it was said that he loved the tall
deer as if he were their father; the deer of
Exmoor have hundreds of such fathers, for
they are loved by every one. Red deer are
a passion with rich and poor. Farmers,
large and small, hunt and aid the hunt in
every possible manner, and besides those
who have horses numbers follow on foot.

Deer are extremely nervous at the sound
of a gun. A single report will drive them
all away, and as the echo rolls along the
wooded hills every stag will start. Those
whose orchards are entered by the deer
sometimes fire off a gun to drive them
away, the noise being sufficient. Though

so timid in some ways, and especially by day, the deer are not easily alarmed from food that pleases them. If a man gets out of bed and drives them out of the orchard —their raids are generally made at night— they will very soon return after he has retired. In fact, it is almost impossible to keep them out of places to which they have taken a fancy.

There are some very large covers near Porlock running along the coombes—altogether nine miles of oak woods. Anywhere else but on Exmoor, where everything is on a large scale, and distance is the most marked feature, nine miles of woods would be called a forest. On Exmoor a forest is only a cover. In these great covers the deer have taken up their residence, and have so increased that at last the damage they have done has led to efforts being made to force them out. Besides the injury to the

adjacent crops, where so many deer are
gathered in one place, the stags destroy the
young firs in the plantations. Rubbing their
heads against the young trees to wear off
the velvet, their antlers not only bark the

porlock
Weir

trees but splinter the branches. The sap-
lings are thus completely broken to pieces,
and of course will not grow. The gamekeepers have deerhounds to hunt them out
of the covers, and yet even with these they

find it impossible to drive the deer away. Blank cartridges will have to be used; perhaps even that will not be effectual. The persistence with which the deer keep in these great woods is inimical to the interests of the hunt.

When a meet takes place the stag will not break cover, and hours are lost while he runs to and fro in the wood. So many stags herding together make it difficult to single one out for a run, the hounds divide, and the day is half gone before the chase begins. Could the deer be got out of the forest to live more in the heather on the hills it would be an advantage. Damage to the crops is more serious when concentrated in a locality, and, of course, if a large herd of deer remain in a wood they will feed on whatever is nearest. But they are not to be moved without difficulty; they are most capricious in their likes and dislikes, and have been compared in this respect to moles. One day a mole-hill appears suddenly in a field; another is immediately thrown up, a third, a fourth, whole rows of mole-hills; nor can trapping exterminate them. After awhile the moles go on, and desert the place. Deer used to lie a great deal at Slowby, and do not now so much. Haddon Hill is a favourite locality; yet in the spring of the present year [1884] numbers of them had gone across to Hawkridge. They go where they like and stop where they like.

The damage they do to crops is so extensive that without the goodwill of the farmers stag-hunting could not last a single season. Nothing could demonstrate more thoroughly the enthusiasm which hunting the red deer inspires in those who follow it than the fact that the farmers over such an immense breadth of country should unanimously agree to endure these losses.

Compensation is of course paid, but even compensation may fail to recoup. Beyond the loss of a crop there is the loss of the fertilisation which would ensue from the stock fed on it, and it is not always possible in times of scarcity even with money to purchase fodder. Three losses fall on the farmer, whose crop is ruined. First, the market value of the crop ; next, the loss to the ground of the fertilisation that would have been obtained from its consumption ; thirdly, the difficulty, perhaps impossibility, of replacing the material destroyed. Loss of time might be added, since another crop cannot be grown till the season returns in due course. Unhesitating goodwill alone can explain the continuance of stag-hunting under these risks ; unhesitating goodwill and an enthusiasm not to be matched by that aroused in any other sport. Only, indeed, the noblest sport of all—the chase of the

H

red deer—could excite a whole country to such generous enthusiasm. Deer may be said to eat as much as the small Devon cattle which are kept in this part of Somerset; they feed sometimes with the bullocks that are turned out on the moors.

They will have the best of everything, and roaming about at night select the meadow with the most succulent grass. They enter orchards, too, in spring for the long grass that grows between the apple-trees. Turnips are a favourite food, and leaving the moors they wander miles down into the cultivated fields to find them. The stag as he walks across the turnip field bites a turnip, draws it from the ground, and throws it over his shoulders, the jerk detaching the fragment he holds between his teeth, and which is the only portion he touches. He takes but one bite at each turnip, casting the remainder aside in this way, and his course

can be traced from one side of the field to
the other by the turnips pulled and thrown
away after his snatch. In this disdainful
manner he damages far more than he actually eats. Hinds eat the turnip down into
the ground as a sheep would.

A herd of stags or hinds getting into a
turnip field will eat broad patches and paths
about it. If it is a small field they may
destroy every root, and many a farmer visit-
ing his field in the morning has found that
every turnip in it has been pulled up and
pitched aside by stags in the night. Of
potatoes, again, they are very fond, and get
at them by scraping away the earth with
their fore-feet, or slots, eagerly eating the
potatoes thus laid bare. Carrots attract
them—almost all animals are fond of carrots,
or carrot-tops. Cabbages please them ; they
will strip a garden of cabbages in no time
as clean as possible. It has been noticed

that barren hinds are the most addicted to
doing mischief in gardens. But perhaps
the greatest injury is done to wheat.

Stags visit the wheat fields at two seasons.
They come so soon as the green leaf shoots
up and nibble it, and are especially fond of
it just before the ear appears, when it is
full of succulent juices, and pleasant even
to a human palate. Any one who will pull
a green ear of wheat and crush the stalk
between the teeth will find it sweet to taste.
As it turns yellow and becomes drier, more
like straw, they leave it, but return again
when the ears are ripe. Immediately before
harvest they will go into a wheat field and
remain there day and night for a week
together. Eight or ten stags may herd in
a field and eat and destroy fifteen or twenty
pounds' worth before discovered. The wheat
fields are often far from the homesteads,
and not very frequently visited; the stags

lie down in the daytime, and the wheat,
then at its highest, hides them.

The colour of their red-gold coats shades
well with the ripe corn, and, unless their
antlers or their marks be seen, they may
be unnoticed if any one does pass. They
do not bite the ears of wheat off, but take
three or four straws at once in the mouth
and lift their heads, drawing the ears through
their teeth, and so stripping each ear as if
it had been threshed out standing. There
is not a grain left in the ear, and after
eight or ten stags have been at this work
for a few days it is easy to imagine what
a state the crop is left in. For such de-
predations heavy compensation is paid by
the hunt.

The deer are fond, too, of oats, and
eat them ripe in exactly the same way;
oats strip easily when drawn through their
mouths. They will eat barley occasionally

if there is nothing else about, but not so much; the awn is troublesome to them. They will get into rye-grass and damage it, but very seldom touch a rick of hay. One winter, when the ground was more than usually bare, and there seemed absolutely nothing for the sheep or ponies, a rick or two of hay was pulled round the outside, but this was exceptional. Stags jump so well and are so bold that it is next to impossible to keep them out of anything they fancy, and hinds climb over the highest walls and fences. The beech hedges of the country, as before described, grow on walls, and are high and thick, but these are not the least obstacle.

The farmers place stakes in the hedges, and hang a vine of straw along from stake to stake a foot or so above the top of the hedge. A vine is a rope of twisted straw; this in itself would not for a moment resist the impact of a stag, but the rope is smeared with tar, which they dislike and avoid. This is a protection to some extent where it can be done. In time, as the winter and winds break down the straw rope, fragments of it alone remain, drooping from the stakes among the fresh green beech spray of the spring. Wire is sometimes placed along above flakes in the arable fields. Ingenious scarecrows are put up; the stags on entering the field quietly walk to the dummy figure and sniff it contemptuously, as if they were perfectly aware from the first of its harmless character, and merely took that trouble out of habitual precaution. Some one tried high white gates to frighten them. The first time one of the white gates was left open the stags walked through.

Apples they are extremely fond of. They enter an orchard at night and go through, stripping every branch they can reach, and

stags can reach high and clear boughs farther up a tree than would be supposed.
They swallow the apples without biting
them, just take them from the branch and
swallow at once. Now and then when a
stag is killed and paunched, quantities of
apples drop out and roll about the ground,
the peel not so much as cracked ; the poorer
boys think nothing of eating these as they
find them fresh from the deer, without so
much as washing the apples, and what they
cannot eat they pocket for future enjoy-
ment. These are the principal things the
deer feed on in the cultivated fields. They
go far down into the valleys and plains
for the wheat. When the damage they do
is enumerated it is evident at once that
stag-hunting is a sport of the most fasci-
nating character, or such losses would not
be endured for a month.

On the moors the deer eat the fresh

grass that springs after tracts are burned, the tops of the heather, and the grass that grows between the young firs in plantations. They will eat the leaves of hawthorn and beech, and in the covers are said to sometimes take oak leaves. Bramble leaves they feed on both in summer and winter, and are very fond of ivy, grazing on quantities of the ivy growing along the ground in the woods. Ivy will attract them to a cover, and they grow fat on it. But above all things they love acorns, and devour immense quantities of them as they fall from the trees. It is at the acorn time that the stags are fattest; if the crop of acorns happens to be plentiful they have a perfect feast. Sprays of ash tempt them, the fresh leaf on the young shoots that start up after the old wood has been cut; they eat it off as level as if cut with a bill-hook, stags especially. The calves frisk and play about their mothers

as they feed, and the grown deer are sometimes playful.

In summer they live well and find ample
food, but in winter are sometimes hard
pressed. They pick a little here and a
little yonder; it must, however, be a hard
time for them, especially when snow falls and
lies for weeks, as it will do on Exmoor when
there is none in the plain. These great distances covered with snow are desolate in the
extreme—white distances beneath and grey
sky over. The deer know when the snow is
coming—they leave the hills and descend into
the coombes, and lie there " under the wind,"
as the Exmoor phrase is. The shepherds seeing them come down recognise it as a sign
that snow is approaching. Snow tries them
while it lasts, and is an enemy as it thaws,
for in thawing snow the scent holds so well
and is so good that the hounds run it quick
as fire racing over the dry heather.

VI.

TRACKING DEER BY SLOT.

THE red deer come out of the covers to feed
at dusk, and continue feeding all night. At
dawn they return to the woods to stay there
during the day. A stag generally drinks
before entering the cover, and afterwards
" soils," that is, lies down and rolls in the
water. They have their regular " soiling-
pits "—watery places or shallow ponds—
which they visit for this purpose. In these
they extend themselves and splash and
thoroughly enjoy the coolness of the water.
All round these soiling-pits there are signs
of deer—their slot or footprints ; and as the
water is always shallow, the stag often covers
his sides with mud, which when he leaves

the pond and goes into the wood is rubbed off against the bushes.

His "bed"—the space he selects to lie in for the day—is usually on the most level piece of ground he can find in the copse. He does not mind if it is a little damp, so long as it is level. He merely lies down like a bullock, and makes no nest as a fox will, turning round and round till the grasses are fitted to his body. But as the stag will lie in the same place day after day, there is a depression in the fern or grasses corresponding to his size. When he has settled himself down he is said to be "in harbour," and it is curious that if once a stag has chosen a part of the copse, the next that comes will generally go and lie very near the same spot, though the first stag may have left it weeks.

Hot summer weather makes a stag pant, and it is often possible to hear him blowing and knocking the flies off in the heat of

the day. Two or three times in the day
he gets up, goes a little way, and returns.
Sometimes he goes down to drink, but always
comes back to his "bed." Those stags that
frequent the hills in the height of the summer
often choose places where the wind draws
through a scanty plantation of trees near the
ridge of a hill. There are seldom any trees,
not even firs or bushes, on the heights of
Exmoor. The winter gales are so severe that
trees will not grow, though they flourish in
the coombes "under the wind," and up to
the very line of the wind. Stags seem in
summer to like the draught of air under
trees, and indeed are hot by nature, and
always glad to cool themselves, as in water.
The day being over, the stag at dusk comes
out again to feed.

Now the work of the "harbourer" is to
find where a runnable stag is in "harbour"
on the morning of the meet, that is, in what

particular copse or part of a wood a stag
has gone to lie for the day, and where the
hounds will find him. It must be a runnable
stag, or warrantable, a term in its strict
meaning indicating a stag of five years, with
not less than two points on top at the upper
end of the antler. Occasionally a stag is
run at four years, but five is the right age.
The "harbourer" consequently has two main
questions to determine, and to determine
with absolute accuracy; first, he has to
choose a stag of the proper age, and next
to fix on the exact spot where that stag will
be at a given time. The "harbourer" must
not say he "thinks" a stag is in such and
such a place, nor that he "thinks" he is
runnable. There are perhaps three hundred
gentlemen on horseback waiting eagerly for
the sport to begin; the pack is shut up for
the moment in a farmyard, having travelled
over from the kennels; the Master and the

huntsman are there ; and no one will brook indecision. He has to bring an accurate report, and must be positively sure. He must not think ; he must know.

Some of the covers, as that at Haddon, reach five miles of unbroken woodland, and it may be imagined that these are no easy questions to answer. The task is often rendered more difficult by accidents of weather, and the " harbourer " has further this to contend against, that, as a rule, he does not see the deer at all. If he can see the deer they can generally see him ; their movements then become uncertain, and they cannot be depended upon. Left to themselves their habits are partly regular, so that the harbourer endeavours to work unseen. His procedure, in fact, exactly resembles the method of an Indian in the forests of America following the trail of buffalo or deer. Feats of this kind described in books of travel always excite interest and admiration ; but the very same thing is done at home in the woods about Exmoor.

Every animal as it goes leaves the imprint of its hoofs upon the ground ; the imprint of the deer's hoof is called the slot, and it is by the slot that the stag is tracked to his harbour. By the slot, too, his age is known, the time at which he travelled along the path, and the pace at which he was going —fast or slow. In general shape the slot of deer resembles the marks left by sheep, but is much larger, longer, and wider. The slot of a stag is at once distinguished from that of a hind by its greater proportionate size, and by each half being longer and more pointed. There is a ridge between the two halves of the hoof mark ; the two halves of the hoof opening somewhat let the soft earth rise up between them. Each half is narrower and elongated and well separated. That of the hind, in comparison, has little or no ridge between, or the ridge is very thin, the slot is not so long, and the outline somewhat heart-shaped.

The broad, rounded end of the slot is the heel, and the points point in the direction the animal was moving. With age the size and length of the slot varies ; that of a yearling is less than that of one two years old, and a full-grown stag of course leaves the largest mark. Practice renders these as quickly distinguished as the capital letters and ordinary type of printing, so that the harbourer knows at a glance how old the stag or hind was. As the stag grows older the heel becomes broader, and as he steps the points of the hoof separate farther, till at five years—when a runnable stag—the marks are wide apart. This enlargement goes on up to six years, and up to that age the harbourer can tell the age with precision. After

I

six there is no further increase, and the age
cannot be distinguished, but as the stag is
then certainly runnable it does not matter.

The opening of the hoof of the stag is
remarkable; as he goes his hoof divides like
fingers stretched apart. The stretching of the
hoof depends in degree upon the pace the
stag was going. If walking the hoof remains
in its normal state; trotting opens it con-
siderably, and when galloping the two halves
are widest apart. By the width of the impression the speed is consequently indicated;
but this varying breadth would confuse the
harbourer's judgment of the age of the stag
were it not for one particular.

One part of the stag's slot never varies in
breadth, whether he is walking or galloping
at his hardest; and this is the heel. The
points spread; the heel remains the same
size. To understand this, place your hand
on the table, palm downwards. The back

of the hand across the knuckles represents the heel of the slot and the fingers the points. Whether the fingers are kept close together or spread apart as widely as possible the back of the hand or heel measures the same across. Corresponding to the age and size of the stag is the breadth of his heel, and it is to that part of the slot that the harbourer looks to assure himself that it is a runnable deer.

The pace at which the stag was travelling is further shown by the depth of the impression. In walking his hoofs sink in but slightly; in galloping they strike the earth with great force and often enter deeply, slipping forward, too, aslant underneath the surface. Lastly, the time at which he passed a given spot is known by the freshness of the slot, and the harbourer can tell if he went by recently—some hours, a day, or two days since. If recently, the slot is sharply marked, and the soil has had no time to crumble if sand, or crack if clay. The bottom of the mark is often moist, compared with the general surface of the ground, for when the general surface is dry it is damp half an inch under. Moistness shows that the impression has not had time to dry.

Till now it has been assumed that the earth always takes a perfect impression like wax ; but in reality the contrary is the case, and the difficulty of precisely determining the age of the stag is increased by the uncertainty of the material on which the impression is left. Deer paths often pass through heather, and they walk on the dry stems trodden down ; these take no mark at all. Nor is there slot where fern abounds, nor on the loose stones which cover so many acres of Red Deer Land. In sand the slot is sometimes almost perfect—

the sand gives a perfect mould of the stag's
hoof, into which if plaster were poured a
good copy would be obtained. But if the
sand has not the right degree of moisture
it spreads, and the marks look larger than
they should. In moist, clay-like earth the
slot, too, is good, and just at the edge of
water.

Weather interferes with slot, especially
heavy rain, which washes it out; nor is
continued drought and heat advantageous,
as the earth becomes so firm it will not
yield. A slight shower is best; in fact, the
harbourer likes the ground prepared for
him, much the same as those who cast pre-
pare their earth for moulding. In judging
whether the marks are recent or not, the
state of the weather must especially be
borne in mind. The right meaning of these
minutiæ is not of course to be learned without long and constant practice; a guinea

is paid for each stag "harboured" successfully. The work commences early in
August, when it is usually hot and dry.
Towards the end of July the harbourer
begins to look round after the stags and
notice their whereabouts. They are then
fraying, rubbing the velvet off their new
horns against the trees. He observes where
the signs of fraying first appear, indicating
that a full-grown stag is in the neighbour-
hood, as the best stags usually fray earliest.

They like the soft-barked trees most to
fray against, and are particularly fond of
willow. The harbourer looks at starting for
the willows, and next to these for moun-
tain-ashes; in the Exmoor country the
mountain-ash is called the quick-beam.
Both willow and quick-beam are frequently
stripped of their bark; the stag pushes his
head against the tree and rubs his antlers,
which are now as hard as ivory, up and

down. A willow or quick-beam not being
handy, he will attack a fir. Next season
you may see such a fir, which was used as
a fraying post, dead and dry, the bark
having been completely stripped from it—
ringed—up to about the height of one's
chest. Deep parallel indentations score the
hard wood where the points of the antlers
have grooved it, as if with an iron instrument, and in these grooves hair still adheres. Numbers of such firs thus destroyed
are cut down for firewood; now and then
one survives, not being quite ringed, and
lives with wide gaps in its bark. Such
softer woods as that of the mountain-ash
are not only barked but broken.

A meet being fixed, the harbourer goes
over to the district on the previous day. In
the afternoon he starts for the covers or
likely places, and if he meets a labourer or
others in the field inquires if any of the

hedges were cut in the spring. To these hedges he goes and looks for the fresh ash shoots which have sprung up since the hedge was cut. These are sure to be eaten off if a stag is about—sometimes a stag will go up a hedge a hundred yards, eating every fresh spray of ash along it. Next he goes to the gaps, or any place of entry into the covers, and looks for slot. He walks round the cover, examining every path and any moist spot he can find. If there is no runnable deer in one cover he goes on to the next, till he discovers indications that a full-grown stag is there. He then considers the condition of the slot, and if the ground is dry " douts " it by drawing his foot over—that is, he obliterates it. The object is, that next time he comes the slot may be new, well-defined, and perfectly fresh, so as to prevent the possibility of mistake as to the freshness of the trail. This part of the work he finishes by six in the evening, and then quits the fields for his home or inn.

He has now got a general knowledge that a stag is there ; but he has still to convince himself by a second observation that the stag will be in his harbour next day when the hounds are brought ; for during the intervening night the stag will go out to feed, and may chance not to return. He now hopes that a slight shower may fall and cease before one o'clock in the morning, to moisten the surface, and so give good impressions. He dreads most a heavy downpour after dawn, which may wash out almost every trace. A slight shower is so useful that he can harbour at once ; if it is very dry weather it may take half an hour to examine a single field.

The stag goes to his harbour directly it is light, and soon after dawn the harbourer starts for his second and final round. If the

cover is small he does not approach it till
he thinks the stag has had time to lie down
and settle himself in his "bed," because if
the stag should be still standing up and
"wind" him, *i.e.*, catch scent of him, he
would very likely move on to another copse ;
but when once settled down the stag would
not shift his quarters for so little disturbance
as that. With a large wood no such care is
necessary, and the harbourer need not wait
for the stag to settle. First he has to
ascertain that the stag has actually returned
to harbour in the same place ; and for this
purpose he visits the spot where he saw the
slot on the previous afternoon. Should there
be a soiling-pit or shallow pond, he goes to
that, and notes the marks in the mud ; or
if he "douted" the slot, he looks to see if
any fresh impressions have been formed.
Dew assists him in the search. When he
has discovered the slot of the stag he tracks

it into the copse or cover, and satisfies himself that he has entered it. The stag being
tracked in, the next thing is to be certain
that he has not come out again, and to know
this the harbourer goes round the copse,
carefully examining every possible place
of exit.

Frequently there are roads or lanes at
one side; he looks at the dust, which will
take a good impression. Instead of going
several miles round the large woods, he walks
up the shooting paths, or drives, and so finds
if the stag has crossed them. There being
no slot across these paths and none at the
places of exit, it is clear that the stag must
be in the copse, and that he has gone to lie
down in his former bed. He is now harboured; and the harbourer, certain of his
game, hastens to his home or inn for break-
fast, and immediately afterwards rides to
the meet to give his report to the huntsman.

Unless he be disturbed, the stag is almost sure to remain in harbour, but it has once now and then happened that he has moved to an adjacent wood. Sometimes a watcher is left to see if this occurs or not; but as a rule, once harboured, the stag is safe in hand.

At the meet the pack is now waiting shut up in a farmyard; so soon as the harbourer comes, the huntsman takes out six or eight couples of hounds to draw the cover, leaving the rest of the pack still confined. The hounds selected to draw the wood are called the " tufters," and are old, staunch, and steady; drawing the cover is called " tuft-ing." At the wood, if the stag has entered up-wind, the huntsman must tuft up-wind—that is, let the hounds go in with the breeze in their faces. If possible, the harbourer takes the huntsman to the actual slot where the stag entered the wood, and the hounds,

"TUFTERS."

or " tufters," are put at once on the trail ;
this is " feathering." The harbourer likes
to " feather "—to set the hounds direct on
the trail.

When that is difficult the tufters work
the wood up the wind, which carries the
scent of the deer down towards them ; a
hound will sometimes throw up his head,
having caught the scent, a hundred yards
before getting to the place where the stag
is lying. But even when they have the
scent the tufting is often only begun. A
stag, if he finds that only one or two hounds
are approaching his " bed," will sometimes
refuse to move ; he will face them with his
antlers, and rather than run in upon these
weapons, the hounds will pass him and seek
another. Though pressed by all the tufters,
the stag will seldom break cover at once, but
resorts to every artifice rather than leave
it. He leads them to and fro the wood :

the huntsman and harbourer follow as best
they may on horseback, and often find
it rude riding, as the boughs are wet with
dew.

A runnable stag always has a younger
companion with him, who feeds with him,
accompanies him, and lies near him in cover.
The two are always together, inseparable;
the younger one is not of age to be called
a stag, but is said to be a young male deer,
or, in the ancient language of the chase, a
brocke or brocket. When the full-grown stag
finds that the hounds, or tufters, are really
following him up and down, he turns on his
friend and companion, and by might of antlers
forces the young deer to take his place, and
break cover for him. This occurs almost
invariably—to cast the hounds off from pur-
suing him, the stag drives out his friend that
he may be hunted in his place. Failing in
this, if the tufters return, and are not drawn

off after his friend, the stag will by turns attack every other stag in the wood that he can master, and force them one by one to break cover, hoping that the hounds may forget him and pursue them. Yet more desperate, he will presently drive out the hinds in order to avert his fate.

Huntsman and harbourer ride to and fro as best they may ; they know what the tufters have roused by the sound. A hind steals away silently ; a stag makes a great noise with his antlers against the branches. They do not ride together, but apart, and cannot see each other ; but the harbourer is aware what the huntsman has seen, or is doing, by the varying sounds of his horn. Holding the horn to the side of his mouth, the huntsman gives short, quick notes if a stag is up and away before him. If either of them has reason to suppose that the stag has gone, from the noise in the bushes, he shouts " Forwards ! "

K

This is a signal to ride to the edge of the wood to see what it is that breaks cover; a runnable stag generally leaves by known paths, paths which he uses at other times, so that it is to these places they ride to watch. When one of them sees the right stag break cover he shouts—" Tally ho ! " Reckless in his haste, the stag does not heed anything in front, and if his path leads through a crowd, as occasionally happens, sometimes knocks over one or two people, not intentionally, nor causing injury, but rolling them aside in eagerness to reach the open country.

VII.

THE HUNTED STAG.

RED DEER are hunted in so different a
manner to other animals, that the term
hunting scarcely conveys an idea of what
takes place. It is a chase, not a hunt in
the sense that the fox or the hare is hunted ;
a chase which has three stages. There is
first the " harbouring," which is finding the
deer ; next the " tufting," which is driving
him out of the wood with a few selected
hounds ; and thirdly, the chase proper, when
the pack is laid on. The tufting may occupy
only a short time, or it may last an hour or
more if the wood is large, and the stag
determined not to come out.

Immediately he has gone away the tufters

are whipped off, so that until the pack is brought up, the stag is not pursued. He has thus a considerable start, and it has happened that an hour has elapsed before the pack could be put on, and yet the stag has been taken. The tufters are whipped off carefully, for if a single hound should escape and pursue he will deaden the scent by running it, and the pack cannot follow so freely. Until the pack comes there is often some waiting about, but when once they are laid on there is a change. If the scent lies well the pace is soon hot, and the country such as tries all but the experienced. A stag goes straight, and has been known to run twenty-five miles ahead.

The elevated table-land of Exmoor is grooved in all directions by deep and steep coombes, or valleys. The side of a coombe towards the bottom becomes rocky, and is often strewn with loose red stones, which chink under a horse's hoofs, and slip and slide downwards. Paths are narrow, and nothing but furrows in the stones and rocky fragments. Very good sportsmen fresh to the country frequently hesitate to ride down, not so much on their own account, as that of their horses, unused to such footing. It is observed, indeed, that the fast hunters of other countries are not so good for riding in Red Deer Land as a stouter, more cob-like, and less valuable horse. At the bottom of the coombe a stream of water always flows, sometimes only a rivulet, sometimes a wide brook, but usually rocky, and awkward to cross. The climb on the opposite side is equally steep, so that a light-built fast horse is soon beaten. Through many of these coombes, which are in effect narrow valleys, there is no riding at all except by certain paths, so that it is necessary either to have a full knowledge of the

country, or to closely follow those who do
know it.

The huntsman who has been riding these
mountain-like paths for twenty-seven years
thinks that the best plan is to keep a horse
rattling along, to let him go, and not to
check or interfere with him. So long as he
is rattled along a horse will seldom stumble ;
he has had but one bad fall in all that time,
and has never been injured. His mare, it is
supposed, crossed her legs going up hill,
curiously enough, and threw him with his
head against one of the stones. His stout
cap saved him. With this exception he has
had no accident, an experience which would
seem to show that with a horse suited to the
ground and accustomed to it, the danger is
less than it looks. But the horse should be
suitable, and accustomed to the ground if
the rider intends to follow closely on the
hounds.

On surmounting the coombe-side there are
miles of heather, and often fair, level going;
the walls occasionally are difficult, but the
risk is from the peaty places. Even in
summer these cause frequent falls, the
horse's fore-feet sink, and the jerk of the
sudden stoppage throws the rider, on soft
peat, however, so that it is rare for him to
be hurt. These places are avoided by those
who know the country—the rough grasses,
sedges, and white cotton-grass giving them
warning. After a stretch of such moorland
may come a ridge of hills, often rough.
Dunkery, for instance, which is the highest,
is covered with large stones. The larger
valleys have rivers at the bottom, which are
often difficult to cross. The contour of the
country is such that by judiciously moving
from point to point, instead of following the
trail, it is possible to watch the hunt for
miles without any trouble; and, on the

other hand, if any one likes he can have as much hard and dangerous riding as he pleases.

It is often remarked by those who watch the hunt from the hill-tops that the pace seems slow. This is an illusion caused by the vast expanse of country which the eye overlooks. There being few hedges, and no trees in sight, and the elevation varying from twelve to seventeen hundred feet, the glance runs over twenty miles in a second. Hounds and scarlet coats seem to toil slowly, moving in the midst of this immensity, as it takes them a long time to cover the space which the eye grasps instantaneously. The pace is really sharp, varying of course with the stag's condition. They are sometimes so fat from feeding on ripe wheat they cannot get up speed—at another time they go like the wind ; much, too, depends on the age.

At the opening of the season the general

hunting is not so good as it becomes in a
week or two. The velvet is scarcely off
some of the stags' antlers (they cannot run
far while in velvet) ; the pack is not settled
down to its work, at least the young hounds
have not, the ground is hot, and the heather
sometimes cuts their feet. As the season
advances the hunting improves and the pace
increases, so that those who desire to see it
in its glory should not go down for a week
or two. Besides hurting their feet on the
wiry heather, hounds cut them on rocks,
and are occasionally stung by adders. A
stag usually goes straight away, then finding
that speed and distance will not throw off
his pursuers, he tries art, next he courses
round, and often returns to bay and is killed
near the spot whence he started. He always
stands at bay in water, a river, or stream,
and very often swims out to sea.

As he breaks from cover, a stag has his

mouth open, blows a little, and lolls his
tongue ; sometimes his tongue lolls out a
long way.   In half an hour or so he gets his
" wind," then he draws in his tongue, shuts
his mouth, and keeps it tightly closed to
the end, while his nostrils are widely open.
He shows no outward sign of perspiration :
he does not " turn a hair," or lather ; and,
however much he may get in water, his coat
never seems wet—that is, saturated.   Wet
does not adhere, as if the coat were oily.

He goes direct at the thickest bushes, if
he comes to a hedge ; or, if it is a wall, to
the highest part, leaps on the top, and then
over.   Now and then he will fly the wall at
a single leap.   He will take places a man
can scarcely climb, always seeming to choose
the most difficult.   Once now and then he
will leap gates, but generally goes through
the hedge or over the wall.   If it should be
a gate, or hurdles, he goes up close to it till

almost touching, and then jumps. If he can find another stag that he can master, he will drive him up so that the hounds may follow him, and lie down in the other's " bed," holding his breath so that the hounds shall not scent him, for the scent lies chiefly in the breath.

The huntsman saw a stag leap up some height from the path, drive another out, and lie down himself in the furze. The stag thus roused took the first stag's place so completely, that the hounds went on without a check, passing close to, and under the first stag. Had not the huntsman seen it, it would not have been known. He called the hounds back, and restarted the first stag, so that had it not been for the man the stag would have beaten the hounds. Indeed, it would seem as if this would often be the case did not the intelligence of man come to their aid.

The stag sometimes runs in among a number of bullocks feeding to throw the hounds off the scent. At ordinary times bullocks do not notice stags who feed by them in the night, but when pursued in the day, directly the stag approaches they set off at a gallop, and by keeping amongst them the stag confuses the hounds. Heated and weary, the stag now makes for a pond or brook, and on reaching it, drinks first, and then "soils"—that is, lies down, and rolls and splashes, making the water fly about. Cooled and refreshed, he starts again with renewed vigour, but still the tireless hounds follow, and at last he takes to the river. The water baffles the hounds, who lose scent in it; but here the intelligence of man comes to their aid; he puts them in the way to find it, and the end is now coming fast.

No more able to run, the hunted stag

" The hunted stag stands at bay in the river."—*Page* 159.

stands at bay in the river, choosing a place so deep that the hounds must swim to reach him, while he is firm on his feet. Though they swarm about him, if the water is deep enough he can keep them at bay with his antlers for a time; but they are too numerous. His strength decreases as their eagerness increases, for they attack him for his flesh; they hunt not only for the joy of the chase, but the savage flavour of blood. Hounds that have not before seen a stag at bay rush in, and are received on the terrible brow-points.

After delivering a blow with his antlers, the stag holds his head high up, his large eyes straining down on the hounds, and his mouth shut. They swarm upon him, and weary him out, pulling him down at last by his legs, and he falls with his legs under him as a bullock lies. The hounds are whipped off, or they would tear him to pieces—their teeth marks are generally left in the skin—and the huntsman comes to kill him. But first, even now, his antlers must be secured, for they turn furiously towards all who approach, and he can kick as hard as a pony. There is a lasso, or headline, kept for the purpose, and supposed to be carried with the hunt; but it often happens that it is not at hand when wanted. One or two of the most experienced present run in, the thong of a whip is twisted round the antlers, and the head drawn back as far as possible, so as to stretch and expose the neck.

Instantly the huntsman thrusts his knife with a quick deep stab—the deer gives a convulsive throb and start, and dies instantaneously. The neck of a stag is covered for some way down from the head with rougher, shaggier hair than the rest of the skin. It is just where this rough hair

ceases that the stab is given. Until within
the last few years the huntsman used to
cut the throat across, high up under the
chin, when there was much blood, which
the present way does not cause. If any
fresh sportsman is in at the death his face
is "blooded," and there is often a scramble
for trophies, as the slot, or hoofs, tufts of
hair torn from the skin, or the tusks. The
teeth polish well, and are set in scarfpins;
the slots are often silver-mounted as the
base of candlesticks.

The eager hounds have the paunch at
once; the dead stag is then placed in a cart
and taken to the nearest farmhouse, where
the farmer usually skins it the same day, the
skin coming off better if it is done directly.
Next day the huntsman comes and cuts
up the carcase into twelve pieces (a hind
makes eight), and distributes these among
the farmers round. The kidney, as a deli-

L

cacy, is generally taken by some old and staunch sportsman. Head and horns are the property of the Master of the Hunt; only a part of the skull is kept without the skin, for it is found that heads preserved with the skin on are soon infested by moths and spoiled. Moths cannot be prevented from injuring them. The skin is the huntsman's; he has it prepared, and skins can occasionally be obtained from him at a guinea for a stag's, or fifteen shillings for a hind's. A stag's skin has the finest colour, but the hind's has a closer hair, and is better as a skin. Such skins should be well shaken from time to time to keep moth from them.

The weight of a stag varies: twelve score is a good weight; some are not more than nine, but the huntsman has killed at fourteen score, or 280 pounds. He makes it a rule to stick the deer personally, in order that it may always be done expeditiously,

and to avoid unnecessary pain. Another
reason is, that he may be sure the stag is
old enough to be killed. The lasso supposed
to be used is precisely the same as that employed in America. On one occasion it was
thrown by a gentleman who had lassoed
animals there. A headline, however, is only
required when the stag cannot be approached,
as when he chances to be in an enclosure;
generally the thong of a whip is sufficient.

But a hunted stag does not always come
to bay in this manner; he often makes for
the sea, and swims straight out, followed
by the hounds, leaving the hunters on the
beach. So common is this, that the hounds,
when hunting is not going on, are taken
down for exercise to the sea-shore, not only
for a bath, but that they may be used to
it. Stags swim splendidly for long distances, and can generally beat the hounds
in the water. They have a great advantage

over hounds—they can rest and float.　They are so buoyant that they can cease striking with their hoofs and yet remain with their heads above the surface.　Floating like this, they rest and gather strength, while a hound must continue using his feet, or drown.

Though the waves be high, the stag breasts them easily, and sometimes swims so far as to be scarcely visible.　After a while the hounds generally return to the beach if they find they cannot head the stag and turn him.　Once now and then a hound over-taxes himself, or is buffeted too much by the waves, and sinks, but not often.　The stags usually take to the sea in the neigh-bourhood of Porlock Weir, and the boatmen are always on the watch when they know the hunt is up.

Four or five fishermen are despatched for the stag, and they row after him, helping any hounds they may see getting exhausted into the boat. They throw a rope round the stag's antlers, and draw him on board, and immediately tie his legs. A stag seems an awkward animal to get into a boat, but they manage it without much difficulty, and bring him ashore to be killed. The huntsman, as before observed, always kills, that he may be sure it is a warrantable deer of proper age ; if it proves not to be mature, the stag is let go. Stags have been lost at sea, and their bodies washed ashore at Cardiff or Swansea, on the opposite coast, drowned after a long combat with the waves. How far a stag would swim if he started fresh, without being wearied from a long run, is uncertain, but certainly he could get over a great distance.

The boatmen receive a guinea for bringing in a stag, and half a guinea for a hind. A hound named "Credulous" swam after a stag, seized him by the ear, and, partly

mounted on the stag's back, was drawn
along a considerable way, sometimes press-
ing the stag's head under water. " Credulous" in one season was twice struck by
antlers, once in the breast, and again in
the hip, and yet he ran as staunchly as
ever. It is thought that the stags in the
woods by the sea swim sometimes in it for
their pleasure at night. They do in fresh
water, bathing in a pool, if they can find
one, in the evening as they come out of cover
before they feed. Water is a passion with
them. The brook, the mere streamlet, the
pond, or "soiling-pit," the river, or the sea
itself, it is always the water, as their friend,
and last resource. By day, if possible, they
lie near a streamlet, and drink always the
purest water ; they visit ponds or brooks as
they run, and come in the end to the sea.

Chasing the red stag requires much endurance on the part of hounds and huntsman.

They first have to travel to the meet, then
there is the tufting or drawing the cover,
next the chase itself, frequently after that
the hounds swim out to sea; and finally,
after all is over, they have miles to return
to their kennels. The huntsman, who is
sixty-seven, often rides a hundred miles in
a day, of course with two horses; he is in
the saddle ten, twelve, and even fourteen
hours. His longest rides occur in the hind-
hunting season, but the work in the stag-
hunting season is often as trying on account
of the heat. So great a labour does the
chase of the red deer entail, and so great a
physical endurance does it demand! But
those who do not desire to labour so hard
can see much of the run without any special
stress of riding by keeping to the upper
ground, and crossing the chord of the arc
which the stag travels.

He usually runs in a circle towards the

close, and the hunt can be intercepted by crossing it. Stags in particular districts have their favourite routes, and generally take the same line; so much is this the case, that, the meet being fixed, an old sportsman can predict the course the stag will probably follow, and even the time the hounds will return to kennel. There are now, however, so many outlying deer, and the deer-country has become so extended of recent years, that it is difficult to say what line a stag may take when the meet is outside the ancient limits. It is supposed that a stag takes the course he has been accustomed to follow at night.

He almost always starts on a well-known path, and follows it for some distance, and his after-course depends upon his individual knowledge of the country. The hounds frequently force stags into districts with which they are unacquainted, and the huntsman

is aware by the way the stag runs if he is
in known or new ground. In the rutting
season—October—stags travel afar, and when
chased next year are thought to sometimes
follow the paths they then found out. Stags
are run occasionally from Dunkery to the
Quantock Hills across a wide belt of cultivated country, probably having visited the
Quantocks in the rutting time. Upon the
Quantocks there is a herd of red deer kept
in an enclosed park.

Before now the wild hunted deer has
passed right through this park herd, but
the hounds, though the park-kept deer were
around them and visible, did not quit the
original scent, following their quarry, and
taking it. The power of scent of hounds is
very great ; they will follow a stag through
hinds, or, in the hind season, a hind through
stags, without losing the original trail. Some
think that the deer have observed that they

are hunted at two different seasons, and that
the stags in the hind season do but just
move out of the way of the pack, while in
the stag season the hinds step aside and let
the chase go by without sign of alarm.

Once now and then it happens that a
stag hard pressed leaps from the rocks into
the sea. Pursued and hopeless of escape,
when he finds that speed cannot distance
the hounds, he returns circling towards the
crags which overhang the Channel. The
paths are narrow, the precipices deep, and
the walls of rock steep, so that if he chances
to follow a path among them he cannot
choose but go forwards; the hounds behind
bar retreat. There is no turning back, and,
wild and desperate in his haste, he leaps
from the edge of the chasm, or perhaps is
in space before he knows where he is
going.

The nearest hound often follows, and once

it was observed that a hound which came up some time after the stag had gone over deliberately leaped after him. In this case neither stag nor hound was seen again. The tide at the moment was rushing in and the waves large—the tide rises high here—and, maimed by their fall on the rocks, stag and hound were washed down by the under-tow.

To be runnable or warrantable, a stag in strictness must answer to these two requirements: he must be five years old, and he must bear his "rights" (that is, brow, bay, and tray), and two on top. He is then a stag in the full sense, and in every way fit for the chase.

The points on top are sometimes exceeded, and a stag at five years may have three on top both horns, or three one side, and two the other. But when a stag of five years carries three on top, one of his "rights"— the bay, or second point—is generally miss-

ing from the antler on the side the three
are carried. If there are three on top both
sides then the bay point is missing from both
antlers. The number of points, too, somewhat depends upon the time of year at
which the calf was dropped; if dropped late
in the year (as happens now and then) at
five years the stag would carry one point
less than another born very early in the
spring.

These facts are not only known from observation, but have been substantiated by
experiment. Captured calves have been ear-
marked, and the marks found several seasons
afterward, so that the condition of the
antlers at a given age has been accurately
ascertained. The horns of those stags that
lie and feed in more enclosed places, where
the food is abundant, have the beam thicker
than it appears on the heads of those that
lie on the moors. When six years old a

stag has his "rights," and three on top one or both sides.

At four years a male deer is occasionally considered a stag and runnable, if he is heavy, and carries two on top both horns, and may be chased if no other is to be found, but the proper age is five. At four years a male deer bears brow, tray, and two on top (without bay, and therefore not with full "rights"); sometimes only brow, and tray, and two on top one side, and upright the other; upright indicates that the antler terminates in one point at the top. These points they sometimes carry at three years, but at three are only reckoned to bear brow, tray, and uprights both sides.

In writing these differences appear minute, but in reality they are marked, and those who have had practice have not the least difficulty in distinguishing the various con-

ditions of the antlers, and deducing from
these the age of the deer.

Such are the points and definition of a
warrantable stag as understood at the present
day on Exmoor. They do not quite correspond in every particular with the statements
in ancient books of venery or hunting as to
the signs of a runnable deer, and the gradual
enlargement of the antlers year by year.
The divergence is probably due to the peculiar nature of the country where the red deer
are now alone found wild in England, and
which, as already explained, is singularly
exposed and cold in winter. Even there a
difference is observed between the horns of
the stags feeding in enclosed ground and
those that lie in the North Forest ; that is,
on the highest moors. The ancient writers,
recording the experience of their own times,
when there were wild deer in every part,
referred to the growth of antlers in England

at large, and not in one district only. Some
of these books, too, seem to contain evidence
that the contents were partially transcribed
from a work originally written in Norman-
French, and probably in France, where deer
may develop their horns in a slightly different sequence. Norman-French may still
be continually traced in hunting terms; the
word " soil," for instance, which is said of a
stag bathing, was anciently written *soule*.

VIII.

HIND-HUNTING.

It is a remarkable fact that hinds run longer than stags. A hind will sometimes run for five hours before the hounds; how many miles she will cover in that time it is difficult to estimate, but the pace is very rapid, and it cannot be much less than fifty, when the doublings are reckoned. One thing in favour of the hind is the season; hinds are hunted in cold weather, and stags in warm—when too the stags are fat. Still the fact remains that the female is stronger, and will run longer than the male deer. There is no "harbouring" in hind-hunting; the information where hinds are to be found is brought to the huntsman by the gamekeepers of the district where the meet is. In the short days the huntsman often begins his work at nine in the morning.

When a hind has been found, and the hounds are following, she not only depends on speed, but gives every possible trouble by doubling. She will go round and round a field, like an old hare, and then leave it by a great leap to foil them. At these breaks of the scent the hounds are checked, and sometimes the young hounds will begin to run it back the wrong way; they are then said to "hunt heel." The ancient term was to "hunt counter," a term constantly found in old books and plays to express the sense of travelling with the back to the object sought. The hounds are then following the "heel" of the deer. Older hounds on coming to a check, when they lose the scent, cast round, that is, make a small circle till they find it again, and some are very clever at this.

M

Sometimes if the snow is deep—not thawing—a hound will thrust his nose into the
slot of the deer as if to question it. The
hind gives the real hard work of hunting,
not only going as fast as she can, but giving
every possible difficulty. If she discovers
that her doublings are of no avail, she tries
to circle round and enter the herd of hinds
from which she was detached. By getting
among them she may perhaps throw the
hounds off her scent on to that of another
hind. Should they miss her in this way, and
take another, they never follow the second
with such goodwill. But if she cannot throw
them off, then, like the stag, she presently
makes for water, and enters the nearest river.

Water carries no scent, so that the hounds
on reaching the bank lose it. Young hounds
in such circumstances often stop altogether,
until they have been taught. The huntsman
on coming up judges which direction the

deer has taken by the point for which she was making. He sends part of the pack across the water, so that the hounds are on both sides, and run along the banks, frequently entering and swimming out to the rocks, of which the rivers of Exmoor—Barle and Exe—are full. The tops of the rocks are often above the surface, and at these they sniff, lest the deer should have landed on them temporarily. A stag has been known to hide himself completely in the water, under a projecting bush, with nothing but his nose out to breathe, and has been passed by the hounds. Here, again, the intelligence of man comes to their aid; the huntsman keeps a keener watch than his pack.

As hind-hunting is in winter, the river is often full, and then there is no doubt which direction she has taken; as swimming in the current takes her and carries her with it, and she floats down in the centre of the rushing flood. The huntsman is always anxious to be on the spot when the hounds run in upon a hind, because, as she has no horns, she cannot resist them a moment, and they pull her down at once. Once when the river the hind had entered was in full flood—stave-high is the Exmoor term, meaning level with the banks—he crossed over swimming his horse, and was obliged to dismount and wade in flooded meadows for some distance beside the stream, encouraging and directing the pack. Presently the hounds found her, but, as it happened, on the other side; he hastened back to his horse, and saw them pull her down as he ran. He swam his horse across again, but when he got to the spot —though it was but a few minutes—the deer was not only eaten, but the bones were picked clean; so eager are the hounds for the flesh of the deer.

The hind, like the stag, frequently runs

at last to the sea, and swims out from the beach. She swims well and strong, and often beats the hounds in the water, though it is then cold. Upon one occasion a hunted hind took to the sea and swam out so far that she was but just visible. The huntsman and one gentleman who had followed close and was with him, tied their horses in cover and watched her from the beach. She swam till their straining eyes lost sight of her; the hounds, wearied and exhausted, returned to the beach. While they still stood trying to catch sight again of the game, a steamer came past, and at this moment the huntsman saw a dark spot on the water which he imagined must be the hind.

As the steamer approached the dark spot it began to move, and he was then certain it was the deer. He shouted and waved his cap, but the men on the steamer did not see the deer in the water—they were

looking at him on the beach and at the
hounds. At last, however, they understood
the shouting and pointing, and saw the
hind floating in the sea. Then began the
strangest chase—a steamer after a deer. The
men on deck shouted and holloa'd, and the
whistle was blown. The vessel easily over-
took the hind, but when they tried to take
her with a rope, she doubled; the steamer
followed, and again she doubled; this was
repeated several times, and each time the
hind, though after a long run, avoided them
by doubling.

Presently she turned and swam ashore,
but here the hounds met her on the beach,
and forced her back again. She swam
straight out till the steamer, which had
been brought in nearer the land, began to
chase her, when she returned to the beach
a second time. The hounds drove her to
sea for the third time—this time the steamer

could not approach near enough to chase
her without grounding, but a hound named
"Trouncer" headed her. This hound swam
faster than the rest of the pack, and showed
greater intelligence. Instead of following
the deer in her windings, he endeavoured
to keep outside her, so as to turn her and
head her for shore. For the third time she
returned to the land, fell, and was taken.

In hind-hunting, the pack often enters
a herd, and divide, some hounds following
one deer and others another, so that there
is much trouble to get them together after
the one chosen, and occasionally two or
three cannot be got back, but have to be
left to themselves. Wire fences are put
round the fir plantations; hinds and calves
slip through between the wires aside as a
hound does, but sometimes they are not
quick enough, and get haunched while half
through; the nearest hound snaps at their

flanks. A hind when started often has a calf running beside her. When she finds that the hounds have really chosen her, she will knock the calf with her head into a bush to save it from them. The calf will lie perfectly still, and the hounds go past after the mother. The hind places her head partly under the calf and lifts the little creature up, throwing it several yards off the line she is following. The huntsman, who is generally close up, has often seen the calf there lying still and motionless, as he rides by.

It has happened by accident that the hounds have chased a yearling, and it is found that a calf will run for a short time even faster than deer, and go straight away, for as the calf does not know the country, he does not turn. In winter hind-hunting is often very rough work. The boughs in the covers are wet with mist and soak the

"A hind when started often has a calf running beside her."—*Page* 184.

coats of those who ride through, and every peaty place is full of water on the moors. Bitter winds sweep furiously across the open distances, driving the rain before them. Vapour hangs heavily on the hill-tops and joins them to the clouds. Rain is often almost incessant, and even those who are hardened to it find of the cold. Hind-hunting is hard work, so that it sometimes happens not more than half-a-dozen staunch riders are present. Those who follow the stag in summer have all the glory; the labour falls to the hardy hunters of the winter time.

Hinds have their first calf in the third year, and afterwards breed yearly, though sometimes they miss. The calf remains a long time with the mother, and a calf and a yearling are often seen running beside her. Now and then a hind has two calves. The calf at first is dappled with white spots, and has a dark line down the back ; after a few months the spots disappear, and the coat becomes of the same colour throughout. Some say that it is only the male calf that is born dappled, but the huntsman is confident that both the male and female are dappled at first.

All deer come true as to colour, and there is no variety, such as is seen in park deer. Until his antlers grow the young male deer resembles the hind, but his chest and neck are much darker. If a calf is found in an enclosure, where the walls are too high for him, he can be easily ridden down. For a long time great care was taken not to kill hinds before they reached full age, but of recent years they have become so numerous, and the claims for compensation for damage so large, that they have had to be thinned. Times have indeed changed since hinds were not killed at all, in order that they might breed, and turnips and wheat were sown on purpose for the deer.

If seven or eight deer were killed in a season it was as much as was expected— once eleven were killed, and it was thought that such a number would never be reached again. But in the season of 1881–82 no less than one hundred and one deer were killed; the slot of the hundredth deer is mounted in silver, and preserved at the huntsman's house. He reckons that there are fifty stags in the district, and some two hundred and fifty deer of all sizes. But besides these, there must be many more out-lying in the broad tract of country they now roam over. Eighty have been seen in one herd; eighty at once crossing a road. Twenty-six stags have been counted together. Four hundred years ago, in the language of the chase, twenty was a little herd, sixty a middle herd, and eighty a great herd, so that the Exmoor herds equal those of ancient times.

Towards the end of the stag-hunting season, as the rutting-time approaches, the stags begin to bellow. From long observation the harbourer can tell the best stag by his bellow; it is not that it is continued longer than that of others, but the best stag's has more volume of sound and is shriller. At this time the stags fight, using their antlers as skilfully as cunning duellists did their rapiers. They feint, and jump forwards, and watch an opportunity; occasionally one gets a stab from an antler, and sometimes in their rage they break their antlers; not always the heaviest stag but the quickest wins, as he "winds" the heavier stag, and wearies him.

The younger stags having shorter horns are easily conquered; they are driven away, and wander great distances in search of a hind ; they travel so much and so far as to soon get thin. The hinds prefer the older stags, and when two are fighting they will sometimes approach and butt the one they dislike behind, and the one they butt is generally beaten. It is said that stags rarely fight twice. The conqueror is master of the wood, and is accompanied by five or six hinds. The stags in a cover soon know their master, and yield ; the fighting is when a strange stag arrives from a distant wood, perhaps having come ten miles. There is then a battle between the intruder and the master of the copse.

At this time a stag's neck becomes much thicker, and is said to be very tough. Some say that when a stag has won a battle, if a man chance to be present he will run at him, but the huntsman is of opinion that a stag never attacks a man, not even at rutting-time. Men are sometimes hurt in approaching a stag at bay, but he thinks that a stag would never of his own volition attack any one. The huntsman has had twenty-seven years' experience of the deer under every circumstance, and his opinion is therefore of value. A stag defends himself with antler and hoof, striking and kicking (at bay), he never bites ; in this respect deer are like sheep. Stags and hinds live separate, except in the rutting-time; herds of stags keep together, and herds of hinds.

At the season when the stags drop their horns the stags separate from each other. Later, when calving, the hinds separate and are seen alone, or but a few together. The seasons on Exmoor seem later than those mentioned by ancient writers on the chase ; the stags do not get their full heads till later. As with other animals, so their ways are local, and these writers doubtless obtained their information in places with a warmer climate than the exposed moors, at a time when the red deer were found in every county. This must be the reason that the date of the antlers becoming full on Exmoor is later than that given by ancient writers. By Exmoor the lesser celandine leaves are verdant and in full growth in the second week of June, yet in other districts the celandine is remarkable for completely disappearing before the end of May. Not only does the buttercup-like flower fade, but the leaves die away, and it is difficult even to find the root.

Deer generally feed with their heads to the wind, but at rest look to leeward. Hunted venison is considered much better food than the venison of a deer that has been shot. But no arrow whistles or bullet sings over Exmoor now—the sound of the horn alone is heard, and the deer are even said to re-cognise the scarlet coat. Is there any time

N

of the year that the horn does not sound,
or that hounds are not afoot after some game
or other in Red Deer Land? There is hunting almost the whole year round; the interval
is so short the staghounds have to be kept in
condition and fit for work from year's end to
year's end.

In spring the otter-hounds are busy in
the rivers and streams. After staghounds are
past the strain and effort of stag-hunting they
are frequently sent to the pack of otter-
hounds. Besides this, there is fox-hunting
and hare-hunting, so that there is scarce a
moment the whole year through that game
is not being chased in the red deer country.
Then there is the black-game shooting on
the moors, the partridges on the corn-lands,
and the pheasants in the woods. Snipes
frequent the peaty places and ponds left by
the removal of the turf on the moors, and wild
ducks and golden plovers are shot. Add to

this the trout-fishing, and sometimes salmon-
fishing, and there is a complete catalogue of
sport.

Yet with all this chasing, sound of horn
and sound of gun, it is curious to observe
that the birds usually found near homesteads
are much less timid than is the case in other
counties. The chaffinch, for instance, will
perch at the very elbow of the trout-fisher ;
the tame pigeons in the village street are
tame indeed, since it is difficult to avoid
driving over them, and there is a manifest
absence of aimless brutality, such brutality
as compels owners of trout streams near large
cities to cover the water over with hurdles
from bank to bank, lest the fish in spawning
time be destroyed by stones. There is a total
absence of ruffianism of this kind.

Something else, too, besides the red deer
has survived, and that is courtesy. Go wherever you will in red deer country you will be

met with politeness, hospitality, and readiness to oblige. If you are thirsty, you have only to knock at the nearest door, and, according to your taste, you can partake of cider or milk ; and it is ten to one you are asked to enter and spend half an hour in a pleasant gossip. Everywhere there is welcome, and the slightest incident is sufficient introduction ; everywhere hospitality, and everywhere politeness. On the road every man you meet, according to his station, nods his head or touches his hat, and no one passes another without saluting. Walk down the village street, and all who are about, in their gardens, at their doors, on horseback or afoot, wish you " Good morning." This is not only observed towards visitors, but amongst themselves.

Farmers salute farmers ; labourers and employers acknowledge each other's presence. The difference is so marked between these habits of personal courtesy, and those that prevail in large towns, that it seems like another country altogether. Nor is it a superficial courtesy, but backed by a real willingness to oblige. Any one with an interest in sport, antiquities, old china, old furniture, finds not the least difficulty in his way, but can satisfy his curiosity to the full.

As an instance of the real goodwill that subsists under the outward politeness may be mentioned the bees at sheep-shearing time. The farmers and farmers' sons at that season visit each farm in succession—twenty, thirty, or more of them together sit down in the barn and shear the sheep. It is a regular bee, on the American pattern, or rather the adventurers from Westward Ho! carried the custom with them across the Atlantic. A farmer who would not assist his neighbour at such a time and join the party would be regarded as a churl; but, as a matter of fact, none ever do refuse.

These sheep-shearing parties soon clear off the work ; sometimes a farmer has six hundred to be shorn, sometimes as many as two thousand. It is one man's work to hand the cider and refreshment round, and there is many a song at night. The sheep wander almost wild among the deer, and are collected from the haunts of the deer for the shearing. They have some habits which resemble those of wild animals ; each party or tribe of sheep, for instance, has its own special feeding-ground, which they choose out of the moor or hillside, and though they wander about they generally return to this place. When shorn the lambs, with their horns made more conspicuous by the removal of the wool, look like goats. Sheep-shearing time is an annoyance to the trout-fisher, as the water is fouled by the grease, called the " yok," washed from the wool, which drives the fish away temporarily.

These bees bring into relief the culture of

goodwill that survives here. Men are not so sharply defined in isolation as in localities nearer civilisation. They do not stand aloof in villa-seclusion, close by and yet divided for a lifetime. Here they acknowledge each other's existence, they approach and lend a helping hand in stress of work.

The common bond of sport has much to do in preserving this spirit : every one takes the deepest interest in the deer, and in sport generally; it is a topic certain to come up, and thus a community of feeling causes a pleasantness of manner. With the red deer of the old-world time of England survives the old-world courtesy and hospitality and the old-world friendliness; it is merry England still. Wild as Exmoor is, and far from the centres of civilisation, there is more courtesy and kindliness in the inhabitants of Red Deer Land than where the right to lead the van of modern life is loudly claimed.

IX.

A MANOR HOUSE IN DEER LAND.

THERE is an old hall with a knight's helmet carved above the porch. The black oak door stands ajar, so massive and heavy with iron rivets, that no gust of air can stir it. A wind comes from the woods, and entering a vaulted passage strays aside freely into the dwelling rooms. For the door in the passage is also ajar, being in like manner of thick oak, iron studded, and unmoved.

Within, the high windows set deep in the wall do but just overcome with all their light the heavy weight of the black oak furniture. Dark oak shutters, dark oak window-seats, dark oak beams overhead, a black table in the midst of the great room, oak cabinets,

and lesser tables; all engrained with age.
The bright light of the summer day, glowing
June, stays at the glass panes—looks in but
comes no farther. It is lighted but not full
of light; there is no brilliance in the atmosphere above the great black table.

There are shadows in the corners and
under the cabinets—shadows that have lingered there these centuries past; the ceiling
is a broad, dark shadow, as if a cloud hung
overhead. A step in the passage sounds
afar and dull, as of some one who had gone
by into the stream of Time. His shadow has
flitted by the half-open iron-studded door;
his shadow only. The grey stone floor cools
the air of hottest June, as the black furniture cools the light. Without, the wood
near at hand is lit up, brightly green, and
the leaves play in the breeze, insects are
busy there dancing their sun-dance, and
chestnut-bloom gleams white among the

spray. No insects enter here through the half-open door—there is no hum: it is silent, cool, and old.

The very polish of the oak is lustreless, it is smooth, but does not reflect. Old shadowy days of rapier and ruff, armour, and petronel, days when the Spanish Main was on all men's lips; of Sir Francis Drake, whose cannon sound still in the hottest hours of summer; old shadowy days, melted into night three centuries since, have left a little of their twilight in this hall. There is a dream in every chair; romance grown richer with age like the colour of the oak —forth from the iron-studded door goes the cavalier and his lady a-hawking.

As the men who built this chamber lived their time in the forest and on the moors, thumbing no weary books, so it is right that to this hour it should be filled with the spoils and curiosities of the woods. A reddish-brown marten-cat, or pine-marten, trapped by chance thirty years ago, is in one case, the very last of the pine-martens, once hunted. This creature, extinct in Southern England, may often be seen in museums, brought perhaps from abroad; but it is rare to find one that was actually trapped as this one was by a living person. There is, too, a polecat, or fitch, with ferret-like head, and an otter beneath; a black harrier, marsh harriers, an osprey, shot at the trout ponds, heath-poult, a long-eared owl, and many others. A kite was shot lately; his wings outstretched were almost as wide as a man's arms held open.

On the top of a bird-case is a powder-flask, and by it pipes in a stand; on the great black central table lies a gun—there are fourteen guns about somewhere, but these are not enough for such a sportsman, and negotiations are proceeding for the pur-

chase of another.   When the fifteenth has
been purchased there will soon be talk of
another, for guns are things you never get
tired of buying and trying.   Under the table
on the stone floor is one of Sir Francis
Drake's magic cannon-balls.   The tale is
well known how he was fighting the Span-
iards, and his faithless lady-love at home
started for church to wed a rival, but at the
altar a mighty cannon ball, shot from over
the ocean, passed between the bride and
bridegroom.   The admiral and magician thus
warned them of his displeasure.   Something
of its charmed character adheres to the ball
still; and if carried away, no matter to what
distance, it invariably rolls back home of its
own accord, and is found in its accustomed
place.   Few can lift, or carry, the heavy
black globe, which has the outward appearance of a meteorite.

Silvery-grey tapestry covers the walls of

Game and Deer - open seasons (dates inclusive)

	Great Britain	Northern Ireland
Pheasant	Oct 1 - Feb 1	Oct 1 - Jan 31
Partridge	Sept 1 - Feb 1	Sept 1 - Jan 31
Grouse	Aug 12 - Dec 10	Aug 12 - Nov 30
Ptarmigan	Aug 12 - Dec 10	Not found
Blackgame	Aug 20 - Dec 10	Not found
Common snipe	Aug 12 - Jan 31	Sept 1 - Jan 31
Jack snipe	Protected	Sept 1 - Jan 31
Woodcock	Oct 1 - Jan 31	Oct 1 - Jan 31
Woodcock - *Scotland*	Sept 1 - Jan 31	-
Duck & goose - *Inland*	Sept 1 - Jan 31	Sept 1 - Jan 31
Duck & goose - *Below MHW*	Sept 1 - Feb 20	Sept 1 - Jan 31
Coot/moorhen	Sept 1 - Jan 31	Protected
Golden plover	Sept 1 - Jan 31	Sept 1 - Jan 31

Deer species/sex	England/Wales	Scotland	Northern Ireland
Red stags	Aug 1 - Apr 30	July 1 - Oct 20	Aug 1 - Apr 30
Red hinds	Nov 1 - Mar 31	Oct 21 - Feb 15	Nov 1 - Mar 31
Sika stags	Aug 1 - Apr 30	July 1 - Oct 20	Aug 1 - Apr 30
Sika hinds	Nov 1 - Mar 31	Oct 21 - Feb 15	Nov 1 - Mar 31
Fallow bucks	Aug 1 - Apr 30	Aug 1 - Apr 30	Aug 1 - Apr 30
Fallow does	Nov 1 - Mar 31	Oct 21 - Feb 15	Nov 1 - Feb 28
Roe bucks	April 1 - Oct 31	April 1 - Oct 20	Not found
Roe does	Nov 1 - Mar 31	Oct 21 - Mar 31	Not found
Chinese water deer bucks/does	Nov 1 - Mar 31	Not found	Not found
Muntjac (see below)	All year round	All year round	Not found

There is no statutory closed season for this species.
It is recommended that when culling female muntjac immature or heavily pregnant does are selected to avoid leaving dependent young.

With 130,000 members
BASC is the

VOICE OF SHOOTING

In politics and the media we are
<u>the</u> voice of shooting.

Whether it's game shooting,
wildfowling, stalking, pigeon
shooting or pest control, we
have the experts to do the job.

BUY THE BEST

JOIN BASC

fighting for shooting
since 1908

01244 573030
www.basc.org.uk

other chambers more sunny and habitable
than this ; some pale and ancient, and valuable, some bright in colour, where Grecian
warriors charge, less valuable and more
showy. Still, even in these rooms, where
the carpets and the furniture are of a more
comfortable era than that which endured
stone floors, even here in corners are fragments of the past—porcelain, and old pot-
tery, and carved tokens of a century since.
But the sun of June shines in and does not
linger at the pane ; the twitter of birds and
the hum of insects, the laughter and shouts
of children come through the open window
with the rustle of green leaves. Bright,
happy life of sunny hours dwells round
about amid roses and carnations.

Another iron-studded door opens on the
great kitchen, where the ancient settles are
still in use. Brands—logs four or five feet
long—can be thrown on the wide hearth.

Upon one side of the hearth is a long ver-
tical steel handle, brightly polished, much
like the valve-handle of an engine. By this
handle the smoke-jack is regulated ; at a
touch a small endless chain depending from
the chimney causes the horizontal spit to
slowly revolve. Looking up the chimney
the smoke-jack fills the cavity, like a horizontal windmill perpetually revolving, driven
by the heated air ascending. In how few,
even of the most ancient houses, are smoke-
jacks still at work. No meat is so good
and richly flavoured as that cooked before a
wood fire.

Coming out at the arched porch under the
carved helmet and the inscription (not only
written in a dead language, but the very
letters ground away by Time), a May-fly
has wandered into the hollow as far as the
sunshine slants. His wings—something the
colour of thin old glass, weather-beaten to a

faint yellow-green—are blurred with darker
colour like egg marks. Rising up and down
in the sunshine, he has wandered hither from
the trout-stream. The old tower casts a
longer shadow now, as the heat of the June
day declines. Many an old engraving is up
there, it is said, inaccessible because the
place is full of fleeces. The wealth of the
land here is in wool, and wool has been so
low in price of recent years that fleeces are
stored and kept season after season in hope
of a rise.

The way up to the woods is beside the
trout-stream ; it is indeed but a streamlet,
easy to stride across, yet it is full of trout.
Running with a quick tinkle over red stones,
the shallow water does not look as if it would
float a fish, but they work round the stones
and under hollows of the banks. The lads
have not forgotten how to poach them ; such
knowledge is handed down by tradition, and

will never be lost while a stream flows ; it
will be familiar when the school-books are
dust and mildew.

They tickle the fish as it lies under a stone,
slightly rubbing it underneath to keep it still,
and then quickly run a sharpened kitchen
fork through the tail, and so secure the slippery trout. They tie a treble hook, like a
grapnel, to a stout piece of twine, and draw
it across the water till under the fish, when,
giving a sudden snatch, one of the hooks
is sure to catch it at the side. Trout can
also be wired with a running loop of wire.
Groping for trout (or tickling), still practised
in the rivers when they are low so that the
fish can be got at, is tracing it to the stone
it lies under, then rubbing it gently beneath,
which causes the fish to gradually move back-
wards into the hand till the fingers suddenly
close in the gills, where alone a firm hold
can be obtained.

The rivers of Somerset have stony bottoms, so that the eels can be seen moving about like black snakes. They glide over the stones at the bottom, exactly as a snake glides over the surface of the ground, and when still remain in a sinuous form. Trout swim over and past them. All their motions can be watched, while in the brooks and streams of other counties, where the bottom is of mud or dark sandy loam, they are rarely seen. There they seem to move through the mud, or its dark colour conceals them. Getting into the water, men move the stones till they find an eel, and then thrust a fork through it, the only way to hold it.

Some distance up the streamlet in a coombe, wooded each side to a great height, are three trout ponds. Ferns grow green and thick where the water falls over the hatch, and by the shore flourishes the tall reed-mace (so rarely distinguished from the lesser bul-

rush). A ripple here, a circle yonder, a splash
across in the corner, show where trout have
risen to flies. The osprey was shot at these
ponds, and once now and then the "spoor"
of an otter is found on the shore. Leaving
the water, the path goes up the steep coombe
under oaks, far up to the green pasture at the
summit. Across on another slope, against
which the declining sun shines brightly, there
are two or three white spots—quite brilliantly
white. One moves presently, and it is seen
that they are white wild rabbits. Their
brown friends are scarcely visible except when
moving. Red deer used to lie in the cover
yonder till they were chased, since which
none have returned to the spot. Beside the
oak wood in the pasture on the summit it
is pleasant walking now in the shade after
the heat of the day.

It is along the side of a cover like this
that the poachers set their larger rabbit-nets

at night.   There is one seized from poachers
down at the old hall.   The net is about a
hundred yards long and a yard or so wide,
made of bluish-green hemp, three threads to
the strand, and the mesh about two inches
square—just large enough for a rabbit to
get his head through ; a very young rabbit
could go right through the mesh.   There is
an iron pin at each end to thrust in the
ground.   The poacher having pushed the
iron pin in, steps a pace or two and runs
a stick in the ground, twists the string at
the upper part of the net round the top of
the stick, leaving the net suspended, and
repeats this every few steps till he comes to
the iron pin at the other end of the net.
In this way he can set the net almost as
quickly as he walks.

Three are required to work it properly,
and the net is placed along the head of a
cover between nine and ten at night while

the rabbits are out feeding in the pasture,
so as to cut off their return to their burrows.
Either one of the poachers or a lurcher next
go round some distance and drive everything towards it, while the other poachers
stand behind the net to take out the rabbits
as they come. In a moment or two they
rush from all quarters helter-skelter in the
darkness, and bound into the net. The
rabbit's head enters the mesh, and he rolls
over, causing it to bag round him. The
poachers endeavour to get them out as fast
as they come to prevent their escape, and
to make ready for fresh captives. They
wring the rabbits' necks, killing them instantly. Sometimes the rabbits come in
such numbers and all together in a crowd, so
that they cannot get them out fast enough,
and a few manage to escape. Once, however,
the rabbit's head is well through the mesh, he
is generally safe for a quarter of an hour.

Large catches are often made like this. Sometimes as many as sixty or eighty rabbits may be seen out feeding in the evening by the head of a cover—that is, where the wood joins the meadows. Besides rabbits a hare now and then runs in, and a fox is occasionally caught. Everything out in the fields, on being alarmed, scampers back to the wood, and the large net, invisible in the darkness, intercepts the retreat. Bluish-green meshes are scarcely noticeable even in daylight when laid in ferns, on bushes, or by tall grass. This net down at the hall cost the poachers two or three pounds, and was taken from them the very first night they used it. It is heavy and forms a heap rolled up—enough to fill a bushel basket. The meshes are very strong and will hold anything. A very favourite time to set these nets, and indeed for all kinds of poaching, as with wires, is after rain, when rabbits, and hares too, feed voraciously. After rain a hare will run at night twice as much as other nights; these evenings are the best for shooting rabbits out feeding.

The poacher who goes out to net hares has a net about twelve feet long, similar in shape, and takes with him a lurcher. He has previously found where hares feed at night by their tracks to and fro and the marks of their pads on the wet ground, as the sand in gateways. Hares usually go through gateways, so that he knows which way they will come. He sets the net across the gateway inside the field, stands aside and sends the dog to drive the hare into it. The dog is a cross between a sheep-dog and a collie, very fast, and runs mute; he does not give tongue on finding the scent; if he did the poacher would strangle him as useless, since barking would announce too plainly what was going forward.

The lurcher is very intelligent, and quite understands what he is wanted to do. On finding the hare he gives chase; often the hare goes straight for the net, but may of course follow another direction, when it is the lurcher's work to turn her, and not let her leave the field except by that one exit. To do this the lurcher must be swift, else the hare can distance him. If he succeeds and drives her that way, the instant she is in the net the poacher falls on it and secures her. Hares struggle hard, and if he stayed to catch hold with his hands she might be gone, but by falling bodily on the net he is certain of getting her, and prevents her too from screaming, as hares will in the most heartrending manner. By moving on from gateway to gateway, where he has previously ascertained hares are usually out at night, the poacher may catch four or five or more in a little while.

But it sometimes happens that a hare
escapes from the net, not getting sufficiently
entangled, and she remembers it ever afterwards, and tries hard the next time for her
life. The marks of the struggle are plainly
visible on the wet ground next morning—
the marks of her pads as she raced round
and round the field, refusing to be driven
by the lurcher through the gateway, where
she now suspects danger. Round and round
she flies, endeavouring to gain sufficiently
on the dog to be able to leap at some
favourable place in the hedge, and so to
get through and away. Sometimes she cannot do it; the lurcher overtakes her, and
either seizes her, or forces her to the net;
sometimes she increases her distance sufficiently, leaps at the hedge, is through and
safe. It is the hedge and wall that trouble
her so; she cannot put forth her swiftest
pace and go right away; she must course

"Leaps at the hedge, is through and safe."—*Page* 216.

in a circle. This is another reason why
the poacher falls on the hare the instant
she strikes the net, because if she does
escape she will always remember and be so
difficult to take afterwards. Several poachers
often go out like this in the evening, one
one way and another another, and so scour
the fields.

A young fellow once, who wanted some
money and had heard of the hauls made
by a gang of poachers, joined them, and
his first essay on the following night was
with a hare net. The net being set for
him in a gateway, he was instructed to instantly fall on anything that entered it. He
took his stand; the poachers went on to
different gateways and gaps, set their own
nets, and finally despatched their dogs. The
young poacher watched his net as closely
as he could in the darkness, ready to obey
his orders. All at once something struck

the net; he fell headlong on it and got it under him right enough, but the next instant he received a terrible bite. He shouted and yelled "Murder!" at the top of his voice, but held on groaning to the net and the creature in it, though in an agony of pain.

No one came to his assistance, for at the sound of his yell the poachers imagined the keepers were collaring him, and snatching up their nets ran off at full speed. Shouting and yelling, he struggled and held the creature down till he had kicked it to death, when he found it was a badger. Out feeding, the badger had been alarmed by the dog, and made for the gateway; so soon as he was touched, he began to bite as only a badger can. The young fellow was terribly hurt, both his arms and legs having suffered, and had to keep his bed for some time. Indignant at the faithless

conduct of his associates, who had so meanly
abandoned him, he renounced poaching. Besides watching the net the poacher watches
to see if a keeper approaches. The keeper
knows as well as the poacher where hares
run, and suspects that certain gateways may
be netted. If he sees the keeper coming he
snatches up his net and bolts, and this he
is sometimes obliged to do at the very
moment the hare has entered the meshes,
so that in tearing up the net he turns her
out, unexpectedly free.

The netting of partridges depends on a
habit these birds have of remaining still on
the ground at night until forced to move.
Roosting on the ground, they will not rise
till compelled; and the same thing may be
observed of larks, who lie quiet at night till
nearly stepped on. A partridge-net is held
by a man at each end and dragged along the
ground. It is weighted to keep one side

of it heavy and close to the earth, and in action somewhat resembles a trawl. The poachers know where birds are roosting, and drag the net over them. They will not move till then, when they rise, and the instant the poachers hear anything in the net they drop it, and find the birds beneath it. Poaching varies in localities ; where hares abound it is hare-poaching, or rabbits—as the case may be.

The most desperate poachers are those who enter the woods in the winter for pheasants. They shoot pheasants, and sometimes in the deep-wooded coombes, where the sound rolls and echoes for several seconds from the rocks, it is difficult to tell where the gun was fired. It might have been at one end of the valley or at the other. The gangs, however, who shoot pheasants openly declare their indifference as to whether they are detected or not.

They simply let it be known that they do not intend to be taken ; they have guns and will use them, and if the keepers attack them it is at the risk of their lives. The question arises whether a too severe punishment for game-theft may not be responsible for this, and whether it does not defeat its object, since, if a poacher is aware that a heavy term of imprisonment awaits him, he will rather fire than be captured. At all events, such is the condition of things in some districts, and the keepers, for this reason, rarely interfere with such a gang. Such severe terms of imprisonment are cruel to keepers, whose lives are thereby imperilled.

The path has now led up by the oak woods to a great height, and the setting sun gleams over the hills of Red Deer Land. It is a land full of old memories. It is strange that Sir Francis Drake, like

Virgil, should have acquired the fame of a magician. Sometimes in the hottest noon-tide of summer, when the sky is clear, the wood still, and the vapour of heat lying about the hillsides, there comes from un-known distances a roll and vibration like heavy thunder, fined to a tremble of the air. It is an inexplicable sound. There are no visible thunder-clouds, no forts within aud-ible distance. Perhaps it is the implacable Drake discharging his enchanted cannon in the azure air against the enemies of England.

X.

GAME NOTES AND FOLK-LORE.

PHEASANT-POACHERS go to the centre of a copse, in which they know there are plenty of birds, and make pheasant-creeps. The pheasant is a bird which runs a great deal, and prefers to creep through bushes rather than to fly over. They make tracks through the undergrowth in the copse, and it is across these favourite paths that the poachers form artificial creeps. Briars are pulled down and bent over, bushes broken, or cut half through, so that they will bend, boughs dragged down, and a hedge constructed in the middle of the cover.

Through this hedge they leave holes, or " creeps," for the pheasants to run through,

P

and in these holes place wires with loops to draw up, and hold the pheasant. As the pheasant passes under the creep he puts his neck in the noose, and draws it so that he is caught. The wires are muzzled, so that the bird shall not be strangled. If the loop was left to draw up tightly without a check, the pheasant, pulling against the noose, would hang himself, and be soon dead. But as a pheasant sells best alive the poachers do not want this, and so arrange the loop that it shall only draw up to a certain point, sufficient to hold the bird fast, but not to injure it.

They next go round to one end of the copse—the wired "creeps" being in the centre—and proceed to drive the pheasants towards the wires by tapping two pieces of stick together, or a couple of stones. At this sound the pheasants begin to run away from it along their accustomed paths. Too

much noise would cause them to rise, but
this peculiar tap, tapping merely makes
them run. In pheasant-shooting, when the
keepers wish the pheasants to avoid certain
exits from the covers, and to direct them
towards points where sportsmen are placed,
they set men with two sticks to knock together in the same way, and at this noise
the birds turn back, and run in the direction
required.

Driven before the poacher's tap, tap, the
pheasants presently come to the artificial
hedge, and creeping without hesitation
through the holes left for them, are noosed
by the wires. When the poachers come up
they put the captured birds alive in a bag,
and then go to the other end of the cover
and repeat the process, and so catch all in
the copse; first, the birds are driven into
the wires from one end of the copse and
then from the other. Poachers also look

out for the creeps which the pheasants have
made for themselves over mounds. They
wander a good deal from cover, and especially towards barley and barley-stubble, called
barley-harrish in Red Deer Land. To get to
the corn they have to pass through hedges, and
their tracks are easily found on the mounds.
Wires are set in these creeps, and the pheasants are caught as they go out to feed.

Sometimes in winter wires for pheasants
are set round corn-ricks, to which the birds
resort. All poaching is founded on the
habits of wild creatures. Partridges in
winter also resort to corn-ricks, and are
occasionally shot there by poachers. Both
pheasants and partridges are fond of ants'
eggs. In covers the large wood-ants, which
are about half an inch long, make immense
nests of leaves and fibres, quite mounds, and
to these the young pheasants go and take
as many eggs as they can. The ants often

bite them severely; the pheasant jumps as the ant bites. Where partridges are bred in great numbers the keepers seek out the nests of the meadow-ant, go round with a cart, and dig up the nests, earth and all, and throw them into the cart, and so carry them home for the young birds to feed on.

The woods of Red Deer Land are full of birds of prey inimical to game; the most destructive are the magpies, for they must be considered birds of prey so far as game is concerned. They are insatiably fond of eggs, and also kill the young birds. They are numerous, as many as twenty or thirty being often seen in a flock, and there are sometimes even larger flocks than this. On the moors sheep run almost untended; if a sheep gets on his back in a hollow sometimes he cannot get up, and while in this helpless position a couple of magpies will peck out his eyes. They are fond of the eye, and will take it if they can ; yet the same magpies ride on the sheep's back as he walks, and remove pests from the wool.

The way to kill these birds is to hang up a dead lamb, poisoned, in a tree; they tear the flesh, and are destroyed by the poison it has absorbed. There are always some round the kennels when the hounds have flesh-food ; it is generally hung in a tree, and numbers of magpies come to it. If a shepherd sees a sheep lying on its back he hastens, of course, at once to help it to roll over and regain its feet, for if not able to get up in time the sheep would die. Collies are the favourite sheep-dogs on the moors, and they are very intelligent. A collie was seen, when the shepherd was not about, to run of his own accord to a sheep on its back, and first bark at it to force the animal to fresh exertions. But when the dog found that the sheep, try as much as it would, could not get up, he pushed against it on one side with all his might with his paws, and then with his shoulder, and this pressure was just enough to enable the sheep to roll on to its side, and so to rise.

An eagle seen on the moors could not be approached, but a dead lamb was put under a wall, and when the eagle came down to the carcase the gunner crept up the other side of the wall, and so shot the bird. Hooded crows are also found, and take the eggs of game. Owls are very numerous in the covers. Wood-owls, or brown-owls, as they are indifferently called, are considered by the keepers destructive to game, especially to young rabbits. Rabbit's " flex " is always found in a wood-owl's nest—" flex " is the local equivalent of fleece, or fur— and the bodies of young rabbits have been found in the nest, which is in a hollow tree. They will take a leveret.

A trap for owls is set on a pole; the pole is firmly planted in the ground, and has stout nails driven in each side, so that it is easy to climb up, and fix the trap. There is no bait; the owl comes floating along on his rounds as it grows dusk, and seeing a convenient post alights on it, and is immediately caught. This habit of perching on any conspicuous pole is most fatal to these birds, and however many may perish, the remainder never learn the danger. One such pole and trap was set in a fir-plantation; the trees were young, and the pole was just tall enough to reach above the highest boughs, and so to attract the attention of the birds. Upon that single pole no less than two hundred owls were taken, chiefly brown owls, but many white owls, and some few of the horned or long-eared species.

To draw out an owl from his nest in a

hollow tree is not a pleasant task, even
with a glove on; he will often manage to
get his sharp claws into the wrist. The
way is to seize his head and crush it, killing him instantly, for an owl's head is soft,
and can be crushed easily. The white owls
are not so injurious. Sparrow-hawks and
kestrels are plentiful, and are constantly
trapped. The keepers insist that the kestrel
will occasionally take game, and say that
they have found wings of partridges in
kestrels' nests, though they allow that the
kestrel is not nearly so harmful as the
sparrow-hawk. Buzzards are sometimes shot,
and are now worth something to sell to
collectors.

The vast moors of Red Deer Land; the
great oak covers which would be called
forests in any other country, and many of
which are not used for game preservation,
so that hawks breed as they list; the ranges

of hills, and the inaccessible rocks by the
sea, furnish an endless supply of birds of
prey.   Foxes, too, are numerous; the dog-
fox barks at night in January, and may
then be heard in the woods; the vixen
occasionally makes an extraordinary noise
like the screech of a frightened child.
There are many badgers, and their skins are
often to be seen in houses on the chairs
and sofas. The stone floor of a keeper's
house is carpeted with them; the skin of
the head usually has grey stripes or bands.
One of these badger's skins on the floor
has golden stripes in the place of the grey
marks.

On the distant hills the only break to the
slow curve of their outline is caused by an
occasional tumulus. There are no copses on
the summits of the ranges, only tumuli here
and there, singly or in groups. The contents are not so well known as elsewhere,

" The dog-fox barks at night. '—*Page* 234.

for there is a prevalent dislike to opening a barrow. The feeling is very strong, and those who own property do not care to go against it. It is believed that certain misfortune will fall on the household of any one digging into a tumulus, and that generally a death follows the intrusion upon the ancient tomb. Possibly this idea may be an unconscious memory of prehistoric times, when sacrifices to ancestors and heroes were made in the precincts of tumuli. They were considered sacred then, and the feeling seems to have lingered on down to the present day. Places where battles have occurred, and where human bones are known to lie, must not be disturbed for the same reason.

It happened that some misfortune fell upon a household without any apparent cause; but one day there was found in the house an ancient sword with a gold hilt.

A younger member of the family, free from
the superstition of the elders, then confessed
that he had been digging over and exploring
a battle site, or ancient burial-place, in the
district, and had discovered the sword, and
hidden it in the house for fear of displeasure.
Here at once was the cause of the trouble
that had visited them.

The folk do not like banks; they think
banks are unlucky, and say that the best
way is to have a stocking. Some money is
placed in a stocking, then the owner has
to observe certain ceremonies, and to select
a secret spot, and there bury it. To this
secret store he adds from time to time till
the stocking can hold no more, and in
this way lays the foundation of prosperity.
Many declare that they never thrived till
they resorted to this plan of having a magic
stocking.

The hills are all " knaps," or " knowls ;"

there is one knowl famous for the cure of
hooping cough. The child suffering must
be taken up on the knowl, or hill, and laid
down in a place where sheep have been
folded. The corresponding terms to knap
and knowl for rising-ground are coombe and
cleeve for hollows. Another kind of hollow
in the hills is called a pan. They are
greatly afraid of being "overlooked," that
is, of the evil eye. To be overlooked is to
receive a glance from some one who pos-
sesses the power of the evil eye, and is the
cause of all kinds of mischief. A person
overlooked succeeds in nothing, but is met
with constant disappointment; whatever he
or she does fails; they cannot get on, and
are sometimes overtaken with worse mis-
fortunes.

The wise woman of the hamlet is regarded
with reverence and fear, and resorted to in
difficulty. Much wood is burned in these

places, and for burning wood a hearth is needed, and a hearth necessitates a wide chimney. When the wise woman receives a visit, and agrees to remove the spell, or cast a fresh one, she presently stands in the chimney and mutters her charms to the stars, which at night are visible through it. The hamlet girls, such as servants, continually go to the wise woman; if they lose their money for their pains they are afraid to tell or inform lest the charm should fall on them. In some places it is a witch-doctor instead of a wise woman, and he is called in if anything is the matter with the cattle.

In one village the inhabitants somehow got an idea that a death, or illness, or accident was sure to happen in the place if the clergyman chanced to finish his afternoon sermon at four o'clock. If he concluded at four a misfortune was certain to happen in the village during the next week. This extraordinary superstition was confirmed by several coincidences, which they observed; some illness or accident did occur once or twice, and the belief became firmly fixed. By-and-by the clergyman heard of this, and afterwards took care that the sermon should finish either some few minutes before or after four. As he preached he listened for the warning note of the church clock just before four and timed himself accordingly.

Belief in the wise woman, in omens, and ancient traditionary superstitions, like that about tumuli, is by no means confined to the labouring classes, but shared in by many who are well-to-do and, from their position, would be imagined superior to such influences. Over Red Deer Land modern civilisation has passed like a breath of wind, stirring the leaves of the trees but leaving them as they were. Just as material forces have been baffled in the attempt to cultivate

Q

the wilderness of Exmoor, so the mental forces of the present era have only superficially touched the people. They read the newspaper, and talk the current topics of the day, but their views and ideas remain unchanged. Among the labouring class some considerable polish of language now exists. They converse in good terms, especially the young people, and listening to them, as they reply to your questions, you say to yourself, " This cannot be Zummerzet."

Not one word of superstition, or ancient tradition, or curious folk-lore, can a stranger extract. The past seems dead, and they are not to be distinguished from the people of other districts close to the populous centres of industry. But the fact is that this silence is not change : it is a reticence purposely adhered to. By mutual consent they steadfastly refrain from speaking in their own tongue and of their own views to strangers

or others not of the country-side. They
speak to strangers in the voice of the nine-
teenth century, the voice of newspaper, book,
and current ideas. They reserve for themselves their own ancient tongue and ancient
ideas, their traditions, and belief in the
occult. Perhaps this very reservation tends
to keep up the past among them. There is
thus a double life—the superficial and the
real. The labourer has disused the " z "
openly, but still remains and will remain
distinct from the inhabitants of other counties. It is a distinction of race that cannot
be removed by the printing press. The men
of Red Deer Land are ethnographically
separate from those to the east of them,
and they cannot be taught out of their
racial peculiarities.

A tendency to slur their words is still
apparent; they run the consonants of several
words together, and an unaccustomed ear

cannot divide the sounds. The letter "r"
is rolled and doubled; thus, for work they
say "wurruk," "Burrle" for Barle; beach,
again, is spoken "bache," and wheat is
"wait;" bushes are "booshes;" Dulverton
is "Dilverton." Many old words remain in
circulation or are dropped unconsciously,
and if noticed are apologised for. Heather
is "yeth," whorts are "hurts," among the
labouring people, and to go gathering whortle-
berries is to go "a-hurting." They say
"time agone" for some time since; "right
away over" to express distance, an appro-
priate phrase in a hilly country.

But so complete is the superficial change
that even "plough" has been abandoned,
and is now used in the same sense as elsewhere. By plough was originally meant not
the iron instrument which turns the furrow,
but the team that draws it; they said "Take
a plough and fetch a waggon." The imple-

ment was called a " sull," or " zull "—the
plough drew the sull. The fact of an
agricultural population abandoning an agricultural term like this shows how on the
surface things are changed. Yet on occasion
they can speak the ancient tongue.

In wet weather a man was asked if a lane
was passable—could any one drive through
it? His reply was dubious; he said, "The
ruts be up to the nuts of a leary putt, an'
it would take a good plough to draaw'n
through." Translated it runs : " The ruts
are up to the nuts, or axle, of an empty
cart, and it would take a good team to
draw it through." A lane in which the ruts
were so deep that an empty and, therefore,
a light cart sank to the axle, was not
altogether passable.

Since the schoolmaster has been abroad
in Somerset it is observed that the " h "
has been dropped altogether. Previous to

the spread of education the people were re-markable for aspirating the "h" properly; since they have been to school they have lost that letter. Ancient modes of expression, provincial words, and pronunciation are said to linger most among certain of the older farmers, too independent of purse and mind to change their speech to please the present generation. Curious incidents sometimes happen in outlying places.

There is a church among the heather and woods, and a farmhouse by it; the hamlet is so small that it is not easy to find. One Sunday morning the clergyman was observed to hesitate in giving out the Psalms, and by-and-by an altercation arose between him and the clerk, one maintaining that it was the 21st and the other that it was the 22nd of the month. At last a sturdy farmer got up and declared he would fetch the almanac and see. Out he went, and returned in a few minutes chuckling. "D'd if ee beant both wrong; it's the 23rd," said he. The service having now lost its continuity, he suggested, with practical common sense,

"This be rough riding."—*Page* 248.

"that they shouldn't do no good there now; they had better come on in and have some cider;" and the tale is that they went.

When the Prince of Wales came down to Exmoor to see a stag chased it chanced as the hunt rode over the moors they came to a gateway where the going was exceedingly bad, and a farmer who was passing through at the same time called out to the Heir-Apparent, "This be rough riding, Mr. Prince!"

THE END.